AF333325

ANITA BORGHESE

The Down to Earth Cookbook

REVISED EDITION

Illustrated by Ray Cruz

Charles Scribner's Sons   New York

To Tabitha, Eric,
Marcus, Aaron, and Rebecca

Copyright © 1973, 1980 Anita Borghese
LIBRARY OF CONGRESS CATALOGING IN PUBLICATION DATA

Borghese, Anita.
  The down to earth cookbook.

  Includes index.
  SUMMARY: Recipes for breakfast, lunch, supper,
dessert, and snack time featuring natural foods such as
whole grain flour, dried fruits, honey, nuts, and seeds.
  1. Cookery—Juvenile literature.   2. Cookery
(Natural foods)—Juvenile literature.   [1. Cookery—
Natural foods]   I. Cruz, Ray.   II. Title.
TX652.5.B57 1980   641.5'637   80-21483
ISBN 0-684-16618-6

Contents

Foreword to Parents and Teachers

There is no instinct to guide human beings in the proper selection of food. Each generation learns which foods to choose. The learning process begins with what one eats when young, which is usually a combination of what one's parents provide and what one likes. These preferences are passed along to one's children, and on and on forever.

Parents do seem to know which foods are good for their children. Surveys show that mothers offer foods such as bread, cereal and milk, meat, fruits, and vegetables because "they're good for you." If this is so, one wonders how the crunchy, supersweet puffs known as "enriched" breakfast cereal and the cookie monster ended up on our tables.

We have been seduced into eating foods with little or no nutritional value by the food pushers and their mass marketing techniques. Confronted with a huge and ever-growing food industry that spends billions of dollars annually promoting questionable food products, many of us have become concerned about the foods we eat. Simultaneously, the connections between food, nutrition, and health have become more apparent with the Surgeon General's report on health promotion and disease prevention, which states that the current American diet is dangerous to health.

The American diet has changed in the past years, but it has not improved all that much. We have cut out some cholesterol and saturated fat by using fewer eggs, less whole milk, and a little less red meat. But even though chicken and turkey have become staples in many homes, we're still a "hamburger society." With supermarket shelves filled with fabricated, modified foods, we have increased our consumption of sugar, salt, and fat, and at the same time we are eating less of the nutrient-rich fruits, vegetables, and grains.

The public's health has been endangered by these dietary trends. Obesity is a major health problem, as are the diseases that are linked to it: heart disease, diabetes, hypertension, and some cancers. The incidence of dental caries is a national scandal. That diet plays a role in all these conditions is widely accepted by medical clinicians and researchers. They are considered the end result of what has become known as "the 4 S's": too much stuffing, too much sitting, too much smoking, and too much sipping of alcohol. Part of the solution to this problem of the 4 S's is for parents and children to learn new ways of eating that provide the pleasures of eating well while eating right.

Changing habits and maintaining routines that allow for more nutritious foods, more exercise, normal weight, and less smoking and drinking are a major challenge in the prevention of disease. We can only do this by establishing a supportive environment where families can enjoy good food, explore new ways of preparing it, and share it with others, so that the new eating patterns become the norm of the group. This should help each one of us make and maintain healthy dietary changes.

The Down to Earth Cookbook is an introduction to the new eating style that is so crucial to improving the health of the American public. It teaches good nutrition while introducing wholesome foods and food preparation, not only for children but for beginning cooks of all ages. This is not a diet book but a cookbook of tasty recipes for healthful eating to be prepared from whole, fresh foods that are as close as possible to the way food comes naturally, combined so that they retain their optimal nutritional value and flavor.

Foods tied to the earth can be thought of in five food groups: *

- •naked seeds—for example, grains
- •seeds that grow in pods—for example, nuts and mature legumes
- •fruits—tomatoes, cherries, peaches, and so on
- •roots, shoots, leaves, and flowers—for example, potatoes, spinach, and broccoli
- •foods from animals—for example, beef, chicken, and seafood

Using these down to earth food groups, food prepa-

---

* Adapted from "The Handy Five" developed by Jan Dodds, Ed. D.

ration can be creative as well as nutritious. And what better way is there of introducing nutritious foods to children than to have them prepare the recipes found in *The Down to Earth Cookbook* and learn about good eating as they do.

Marcella Katz, M.S.
Director, Nutrition Division
Health Insurance Plan of Greater New York

GETTING STARTED

Introduction

When this book was first published some children asked me why it was called *The Down to Earth Cookbook*. They wondered what I meant by down to earth. Down to earth means eating foods that are as near as possible to the way nature makes them. All of our food comes from plants, and all plants come from the earth. Wheat, rice, vegetables, fruits, nuts, and seeds, for instance, all come from plants, bushes, or trees that grow in the soil. They're all natural, down to earth foods, so when we eat them we're eating down to earth. When we drink milk, or eat eggs, cheese, chicken, turkey, or fish, we're still eating quite close to the land, because the birds, animals, and fish that give us these foods have grown by eating plants from the earth or water.

Natural foods have good flavor and give us good health and energy because their many nutrients have not been removed by refining or processing, and no chemical preservatives or artificial colorings or flavorings have been added to them.

Down to earth cooking means taking the good, natural foods we've been talking about and preparing them in simple, delicious ways. Cooking them is fun and creative. Best of all, it means making things that are really useful and can be shared with your family or friends. You'll find it exciting to work with foods to see how recipes turn out, and you may find that in following my recipes you come up with ideas for making up some of your own. Your kitchen is a land of adventure waiting for you to explore. I hope to share that adventure with you by showing you how to select, cook, and enjoy natural, flavorful foods.

Some good nutrition guidelines to keep in mind when planning what to eat are: cut down on the amount of salt and refined sugar you eat; eat lots of fruits and vegetables; use more polyunsaturated vegetable oils (which we talk about below) than animal fats (such as butter, lard, or the fat on meat); and eat more fish, poultry, and legumes (beans, peanuts, peas) than red meat. You don't need a lot of meat to have adequate protein in your diet. You get high-quality protein by combining a grain or grain product (cereal, bread, rice, or macaroni) with a legume. Falafel in Pita Bread, Super Peanut Butter sandwiches, and Garden Casserole are recipes in this book that combine grains and legumes. Another way to get sufficient protein is to add a small amount of animal protein (from cheese, milk, eggs, poultry, or meat) to a grain or legume dish—for instance, Granola Cereal with milk, Big Baked Stuffed Shells, or Beefy Baked Beans.

When shopping you'll find it easy to choose the right foods. Fresh is beautiful, and that's the thing to remember about all foods, especially fruits and vegetables. They should be bright, fresh, crisp or firm, and unbruised. Usually the younger and smaller vegetables are, the better they taste. Don't overcook vegetables. They're best if you cook them until they're just tender and still a tiny bit crisp. Sometimes, when you can't locate certain fresh foods, you'll have to buy them frozen or in cans. When you do, it's a good idea to read the list of ingredients on the label and buy a brand that doesn't contain chemical additives or too much sugar or salt. (Ingredients are listed in order of weight, so if salt and sugar are not at the end of the list, then there is probably a high amount of them in that food.) Choose foods that are unrefined and unprocessed. You can usually buy them all at your supermarket or grocery store. If you can't find the following items at your usual market, though, you'll be sure to find them at your local co-op food, health food, or specialty food store.

Whole Wheat Flour is made by grinding entire wheat kernels into flour. It's called a whole grain flour because the germ, which is the heart of the grain, and the bran, which is the skin, haven't been removed. These are the parts that contain most of the vitamins and minerals of the wheat, as well as the fiber. In white flour the bran and germ have been removed, leaving just starchy white flour.

Wheat Germ is the heart of the wheat kernel and has a good nutty flavor. It contains the majority of the vitamins found in the kernel and is an excellent source of protein and minerals. You can use either raw wheat germ or toasted wheat germ. Besides using it for cooking, you can mix wheat germ in with cereals, sprinkle it on ice cream or desserts, stir it into soups, and toss it into salads.

Unbleached Enriched White Flour is wheat flour from which the germ and bran have been removed. Usually four of the many minerals and other nutrients removed from the flour have been put back. No chemical has been used to bleach the flour.

Buckwheat Flour is a whole grain flour made from buckwheat, a grain with triangular-shaped seeds that produce a dark-colored flour of bold flavor. It's higher in fat and lower in protein than wheat and contains useful minerals. Buckwheat is usually mixed with wheat flour so its flavor won't be too strong.

Brown Rice is unrefined white rice. The outer brown covering that has been left on contains vitamins, minerals, and lots of flavor.

Tahini is ground sesame seed. It has a texture similar to peanut butter and has a nice nutty flavor. If you don't find it in the stores already mentioned, look in a store that sells Greek or Middle Eastern foods.

Honey is made by bees from flower nectar and is a good sweetener to use because it's a natural food that doesn't need to be refined as sugar does, and it supplies a small amount of minerals. **Molasses** is a very good sweetner to use because it supplies you with iron. The darker the molasses, the more iron it contains. Unsulphured molasses is preferable to sulphured molasses.

Turbinado Sugar light brown in color, and **Brown Sugar,** either light or dark, are all sugars that have been refined as little as possible and therefore retain some of their minerals. White sugar has no minerals at all.

Sea Salt is made by evaporating ocean water, which contains salt and rich minerals from the sea. These minerals are not found in ordinary table salt. **Iodized Salt** is salt to which an iodine compound has been added in order to help prevent a disease called goiter. If you live in an area where people sometimes get goiter it's a good idea to use iodized salt. You can find out if you live in such an area by asking your family doctor or calling your local health department. Whichever salt you use, try not to use too much, because it can hide the flavor of the food you really want to taste, and your body doesn't need much added salt anyway.

Seeds such as sunflower seeds, sesame seeds, pine nuts (which are really the seeds of certain pine cones), and pumpkin seeds are good sources of protein, minerals, and other nutrients. They're generally used in place of, or in combination with, nuts, which are also high in food value.

Polyunsaturated Vegetable Oils such as safflower, soy, corn, sunflower, and sesame contain essential fatty acids, which you need for development of body tissues. The label on the bottle should say "pressed," "crude," or "unrefined"; otherwise the oils have been refined and bleached and may have had chemicals added before bottling. The benefits you can get from liquid vegetable oils cannot be gotten from more solid cooking fats such as chicken fat, lard, or coconut oil. If you use sesame oil try only a little at first because sometimes it has quite a strong nutty flavor, and you may want to use it along with another kind of oil.

Soft Margarine contains more polyunsaturated fat than does stick margarine, and is preferable to use. It is usually made from safflower, soy (soybean), or corn oil, but may also be made from sunflower oil, or may contain some cottonseed oil. The first ingredient listed on the package should be liquid oil.

Carob Powder is a brown powder made by grinding up the pods of the carob tree. It tastes almost like chocolate and contains a good quantity of vitamins and minerals. Carob is better than chocolate because it doesn't destroy the calcium in the food you've eaten the way chocolate can do.

Happy cooking, good eating, and good health!

ANITA BORGHESE

Here's What You Do First

Choose a recipe and read it all the way through so you'll understand it. Check to see if you have all the ingredients you need so you can shop for anything that's missing.

Ask if it's all right to use the kitchen. Decide whether you want to use the top of the stove or the oven or an appliance like the electric blender, mixer, or waffle iron—so that someone can help you to turn them on and off and to use them properly.

Wash your hands and put on an apron or tuck a clean towel into your belt.

Bring out the ingredients you'll need and the utensils you'll be using and put them all together where you're going to work.

Have some good thick potholders or oven mitts ready to use. Use them every time you pick up a pot or pan from the stove and every time you take something out of the oven or broiler.

If you have a timer, put it where you can use it. It will help you to bake or cook things the right length of time.

If your recipe asks for a pan to be greased, do it before you start to cook.

Remember to keep pan handles on the stove turned in so they don't stick out over the edge of the stove where you might bump into them.

These Are the Cooking Utensils You'll Use Most Often

Apple Corer is a hollow metal cylinder with a handle. You hold the handle and push the metal part down through the center of an apple to take out the core.

Baking Pans or **Baking Dishes** are used in the oven or under the broiler. They come in different sizes and can be round, square, or rectangular. They're made of aluminum, stainless steel, or oven-proof glass.

Broiler Racks are grooved metal racks used to cook things directly under the broiler. They have openings to allow for drainage of fat if you're broiling meat, and they're usually placed over a solid pan to catch the drippings. You can also buy disposable broiler pans that require no drip pan. **Broiler Pan** is any shallow flat metal pan that will fit easily under the broiler.

Cake Tester is a little wire rod or a clean wooden toothpick that you stick into the center of cake or bread to see if it's finished baking. If the tester comes out dry, you know your cake or bread is ready.

Casseroles and **Dutch Ovens** are for baking things like meat dishes, baked beans, or macaroni and cheese, or for serving things that you've cooked in a saucepan—like vegetables. Casseroles come in many sizes and shapes and can be made of earthenware, oven-proof glass, or porcelain-coated iron, which can also be used on top of the stove. Dutch ovens are like casseroles, but they have very high lids.

Colander. To drain liquid off ingredients pour them into a colander and the liquid will run out of the holes. If it's a liquid you don't want to use, set the colander in the kitchen sink. If it's a liquid you want to use in a recipe, put the colander over a bowl to catch the liquid.

Cookie Cutters come in lots of different shapes. Use them to make fancy sandwiches, toast, and cookies.

Cookie Sheets are used to bake cookies in the oven. You can put cookie sheets under the broiler too if you want to brown things quickly.

Cooking Spoons and **Cooking Forks** are big. They have long handles and are made of metal or wood.

Custard Cups are made of oven-proof glass or earthen-ware. They're handy for things like separating eggs or mixing a few spoonsful of ingredients together. You can also bake custards and other foods in them.

Egg Beater or **Rotary Beater** is hand operated. Use an egg beater for beating eggs or whipping cream. Turn the handle very fast.

Electric Blender has a tall glass container into which you pour ingredients you want to blend together

quickly and thoroughly. Blades at the bottom of the glass container whirl around to mix and grind up the ingredients in a few seconds. Always put the cover on top of the glass container before you turn on the blender and always turn off the blender before you remove the cover. *Be sure to ask an adult to help you use the blender properly.*

Electric Mixer is used for things like beating egg whites or mixing cake batter or cookie dough. It has a bowl that sits on a stand and beaters that you lower into the bowl when you want to start beating. The beaters look very much like egg beaters. *Ask an adult to show you how to use the electric mixer properly.*

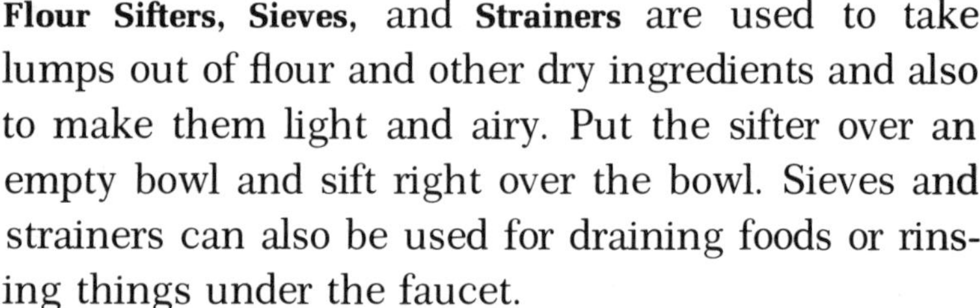

Flour Sifters, Sieves, and **Strainers** are used to take lumps out of flour and other dry ingredients and also to make them light and airy. Put the sifter over an empty bowl and sift right over the bowl. Sieves and strainers can also be used for draining foods or rinsing things under the faucet.

Juice Squeezer is used to make orange juice or lemon juice. Cut the fruit in half and push it down and turn it back and forth on the squeezer part until all the juice has come out. Remove the seeds with a spoon.

Kitchen Knives. Paring Knives have short blades and are used for peeling and paring fruits and vegetables, scraping carrots, and cutting up small things. **Chef's**

Knives look like large paring knives. The handles and blades are both longer. Use chef's knives for things like chopping nuts, slicing tomatoes or onions, and cutting up carrots. **Bread Knives** have blades made especially for slicing through bread without tearing it. **Carving Knives** have long sharp blades designed to cut through meats smoothly. When you want to cut something with a knife put the object on a cutting board and hold it while you cut. Don't hold it up in the air and try to cut it.

Measuring Cups often come in sets. There's a separate cup for ¼ cup, ⅓ cup, ½ cup, and 1 cup. These are for dry ingredients, and the measurement is marked on each cup. There's also a measuring cup for liquids that has all these measurements marked on one cup, as well as a mark for ⅔ cup and a ¾ cup. You can measure any amount by filling it up to the right mark.

Measuring Spoons come in sets. There's a separate spoon for ¼ teaspoon, ½ teaspoon, 1 teaspoon, and 1 tablespoon. The measurement is marked on the handle of each spoon.

Meat Grinder is used for grinding up nuts, dried fruits, and meats. Most grinders have a fine blade, a medium blade, and a coarse blade, and you can put on whichever blade your recipe asks for. *Ask an adult to help you when you use the meat grinder.*

 **Mixing Bowls** are used to mix and stir things together.

 **Muffin Tins** are used for baking cupcakes and muffins.

 **Pastry Blender** helps you blend flour or other dry ingredients into butter or other fats.

 **Pastry Brush** is used to brush liquids onto foods evenly.

 **Pots** are like giant saucepans with handles on two sides. You need two hands to pick up a pot when it's full. You use pots to cook things like macaroni, cabbage, and corn on the cob.

 **Rolling Pin** or **Mortar and Pestle.** Rolling pins are usually used to roll out pastry and dough, but you can also use them for crushing or breaking up nuts, hard candies, or toast for crumbs. You can use a wooden mortar and pestle to do the same jobs. Put a little at a time in the mortar and pound it with the pestle.

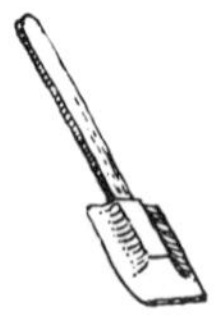 **Rubber Spatula** is good for lots of jobs like scraping things out of bowls and smoothing the top of cake batter.

 **Saucepans** come in many different sizes. Use them for cooking vegetables, soups, and other things on top of the stove.

 **Shredder/Grater.** Use this when you want to shred or grate cheese, carrots, orange peel, or lemon peel. Set the utensil on a piece of waxed paper. Hold the grater with one hand and rub the cheese or other

food against it with the other. Be careful of your fingers when you get near the end. Use the coarse side for cheese and carrots, and the fine side for orange or lemon peel. Grate only the colored part of the fruit rind, not the white because it tastes bitter.

Skillets are wide, shallow pans and you use them on top of the stove for frying, sautéing, or browning things like hamburgers, eggs, bacon, and onions.

Spatula or **Pancake Turner.** These are good for turning pancakes or hamburgers or lifting cookies off a cookie sheet.

Vegetable Brushes have stiff bristles and are used for washing vegetables like carrots or celery.

Vegetable Peeler or **Potato Peeler** is used to scrape the skin off vegetables like carrots and cucumbers, and to take the peel off fruits like apples and pears. If you don't have a peeler you can use a paring knife instead.

Whisks can be used for beating eggs or egg whites, or for stirring sauces on the stove.

Wire Rack or **Cake Rack.** When you bring baked things out of the oven, put them on a wire rack so the air can get all around them and cool them.

Most Recipes Will Tell You to Do Some of These Things

Mix or **Blend**

To stir things together with a spoon.

Cream

To soften margarine by working it against the inside of the bowl with a spoon, stirring it until it is quite soft and creamy.

Sift

To put through a flour sifter or a sieve.

Toss

To mix lightly and gently.

Measure

To put an ingredient into a measuring cup or measuring spoon until you have the amount called for in the recipe.

Measure Flour

When you measure flour, don't press it down. Spoon it lightly into the cup and push off the extra flour with a spatula.

Measure Boiling Water

Put an oven-proof glass or metal measuring cup on the table. Pour boiling water into it. Pick up the cup with a potholder.

Grease

To put a little shortening or margarine on a paper towel and rub it on the inside of a baking pan.

Bake

To cook in the oven.

Blend with Pastry Blender

Push pastry blender down and through ingredients until they look crumbly.

Knead Bread Dough

Sprinkle a little flour on pastry board or wooden work-table. Place ball of dough on the flour. Flour the heels and palms of your hands. Press the dough down once with the heels of your hands. Give the dough a slight turn, about a quarter of the way around. Fold it in half toward you, and press again with the heels of your hands. Continue turning, folding, and pressing for about 10 minutes, or as long as the recipe tells you. You should do this in a nice rhythmical way. If you need more flour as you knead, sprinkle a little on the board. When you have kneaded the dough enough, it should not stick to the board and it should look smooth and feel elastic.

Sauté

To cook in a small amount of oil, margarine, or other fat, in a skillet on top of the stove.

Brown

To cook until the food is brown.

Boil

To cook a liquid over high heat until big bubbles form on the top.

Simmer

To boil very slowly over low heat.

Melt

To heat slowly in a saucepan or skillet until the ingredient becomes a liquid.

Broil

To cook in the oven under the broiler.

Test Meat

Stick a cooking fork in the center of cooked meat to see if it's done. If it goes in easily and feels tender or soft, it's ready to eat.

Break an Egg

Crack the eggshell on the edge of a little bowl or custard cup or other strong cup and let the egg drop into the bowl or cup. Throw the shell away.

Cook Dried Beans (such as kidney beans or chick peas)

Sort out the beans and discard any withered or darkened ones and any stones or other material you may find with the beans, then rinse in a strainer under cold running water. Place beans in a large bowl. Pour enough cold water over them to cover by at least 2½ inches. Let the beans soak overnight or about 12 hours. Transfer the beans and water to a large pot and bring to a boil. Lower flame and let the beans simmer gently 1 to 2 hours until done. Test the beans after 1 hour and every half hour after that by removing a bean with a long-handled spoon and sticking it with a sharp-tined fork to see if it's tender. When done, remove beans from pot with a slotted spoon.

Chop or Slice Onions

Put the onion on a cutting board and cut off each end with a knife. Pull off the outer brown skin with your fingers. Cut the onion in half. Lay halves on board with flat sides down. Cut them into slices. For chopped onions cut the slices into small pieces.

Chop Garlic

With a paring knife cut the end off a garlic clove. Peel off the skin. Put the garlic clove on a cutting board and cut it into slices. Chop the slices into small pieces.

Cut Green Peppers into Strips or Squares or Chop Them

Rinse the green pepper and dry it. Lay it on a cutting board and cut it in half. Pull off the stem and seeds and cut out the white part with a paring knife and throw away. Cut the green part crosswise into narrow strips or cut into squares. For chopped peppers, cut the strips into little pieces.

Cube

To cut into many little squares of the same size.

Core

To take the core out of a piece of fruit, usually an apple. Set the apple on a cutting board. Push an apple corer straight down through the center of the apple and pull out the core. If the core doesn't come out with the corer, push it out of the apple with your finger or the handle of a spoon. If you don't have an apple corer, you can cut the apple in quarters and cut out the core with a paring knife.

Turn Out onto Wire Rack

Remove baked bread or cake from oven and set the pan on the worktable. Set a wire rack on top of the pan. With a potholder or oven mitt on each hand grasp the pan and rack together, one hand at each end, and turn them over. Set them down on the table—the rack will now be on the bottom. Lift the pan off the cake. (If it doesn't come right off, tap the bottom of the pan sharply with a wooden spoon to loosen it.) With potholders turn the bread right side up on the rack and allow it to cool.

Separate an Egg

To take the white and yolk away from each other, crack the eggshell on the edge of a little bowl or cup. With both hands hold together the two halves of the shell. Pull them apart at the top and tip them slightly to let the white fall into the bowl. The yolk will stay in one of the shell halves. Put it in a separate bowl or cup. *The first time you do this, ask someone to help you.*

When You've Finished Cooking

Turn off the stove or oven right away.

Serve what you've made in pretty dishes or on a nice serving plate. Everyone will enjoy your cooking more if you serve it nicely, and it will be more fun for you too.

Eat!

Clean up the kitchen and put away everything you've used.

If you have leftover food, put it in a sealed container or wrap it in plastic wrap. Store it in the refrigerator if it's meat, vegetables, fruit, or soup. Dry foods like cookies, bread, cereal, or other baked goods can be stored in containers and put in the pantry or cupboard.

BREAKFAST DISHES

Yogurt-Cheddar Pancakes

INGREDIENTS	UTENSILS
½ cup plain yogurt	shredder/grater (see page 26)
1 egg	small bowl
2½ tablespoons whole wheat flour or unbleached enriched white flour	mixing spoon
1 cup coarsely grated Cheddar cheese	egg beater or whisk
1 tablespoon safflower, soy, or corn oil soft margarine	large skillet
	measuring cups
	measuring spoons
	pancake turner

Grate the cheese. Break the egg into small bowl and beat lightly. Stir in the yogurt. Stir in the flour. Stir in the cheese.

Heat margarine in a skillet over medium flame. Drop batter into skillet using 1 tablespoon batter for each pancake. Make 6 pancakes at a time. When pancakes begin to brown around the edges and make little bubbles all over the surface, turn them over. Brown the other side. Put the pancakes on a plate. Add a little more margarine to the skillet if necessary to cook the rest of the pancakes. Put them on another plate.

Serve plain or with honey, maple syrup, or Honey Bee Butter (page 43). Some people like salt and pepper on these pancakes, so put salt and pepper on the table, too.

Makes 2 servings.

Granola Cereal

<table>
<tr><td>

INGREDIENTS

2 *cups oatmeal*
⅓ *cup wheat germ*
½ *cup millet flakes*
¼ *cup turbinado sugar or*
  firmly packed brown
  sugar
¼ *teaspoon sea salt or*
  iodized salt
2 *tablespoons safflower,*
  soy, or corn oil
¼ *cup unsweetened*
  flaked coconut
¼ *cup chopped almonds*
¼ *cup sesame seeds*
½ *cup raisins*

</td><td>

UTENSILS

large bowl
measuring cups
measuring spoons
cooking spoon
cookie sheet
chef's knife
large glass jar with lid

</td></tr>
</table>

Turn on oven to heat at 250°.

Mix together in a bowl the oatmeal, wheat germ, millet flakes, sugar, and salt. Sprinkle with oil and toss well. Spread out on cookie sheet and place in oven. Bake 45 minutes, stirring once during baking. While cereal is baking, chop the almonds.

Remove from oven and add coconut, almonds, and sesame seeds. Toss mixture with spoon and return to oven for another 15 minutes.

Remove from oven. Stir in raisins. Let mixture cool, and store in glass jar. Eat cold with milk in a cereal bowl.

Makes about 4½ cups.

Prunella Muffins

INGREDIENTS
½ *cup safflower, soy, or corn oil soft margarine*
½ *cup turbinado sugar or firmly packed brown sugar*
2 *eggs*
⅔ *cup milk*
⅔ *cup pitted, cut-up prunes*
1 *cup whole wheat flour*
⅓ *cup unbleached enriched white flour*
1 *teaspoon baking powder*
¼ *teaspoon sea salt or iodized salt*
½ *teaspoon cinnamon*
½ *teaspoon nutmeg*
½ *teaspoon allspice*

UTENSILS
bowl
measuring cups
measuring spoons
cooking spoon
paring knife
flour sifter
muffin tins
cake tester
wire rack

Turn on oven to heat at 375°. Grease muffin tins or place cupcake papers in muffin tins. Remove pits from prunes and cut up into small pieces.

Cream margarine in a bowl until soft. Add sugar, a little at a time, blending well each time. Add eggs and stir well. Add milk and prunes and stir again.

Sift together flours, baking powder, salt, cinnamon, nutmeg, and allspice and add to the batter.

Spoon batter into each cup until two-thirds full. Place in oven and bake 20–25 minutes or until cake tester inserted in center of a muffin comes out clean. Turn muffins out onto wire rack to cool (see page 32).

Makes 12 muffins.

Savory Swiss Eggs with Anchovies

INGREDIENTS	UTENSILS
1 cup shredded Swiss or Jarlsberg cheese	shredder/grater (see page 26)
1 tablespoon thinly sliced scallions	measuring cups
3 flat anchovies	paring knife
4 eggs	measuring spoons
¼ cup milk	paper towel
dash of pepper	bowl
2 tablespoons safflower, soy, or corn oil soft margarine	wire whisk
	10-inch skillet with cover
	table knife
	pancake turner

Shred the cheese. Slice the scallions and break the slices into rings. Lay the anchovies on a paper towel and pat them dry. Cut them in half lengthwise, then in half crosswise.

Break the eggs into a bowl and beat them lightly with a whisk. Add the milk and pepper and beat lightly again. Melt the margarine in a skillet over a medium flame. Tilt the skillet so the bottom is covered evenly with melted margarine. Pour in the egg mixture. Remove skillet from stove.

Quickly sprinkle the cheese and scallions evenly over the eggs, and arrange the anchovy pieces on top. Put the skillet back on the stove and cover it. Cook over low heat for 4 to 5 minutes until the eggs are set and browned on the bottom and the cheese has melted. Remove from stove.

Cut into quarters like a pie. Serve on plates, using a pancake turner to remove eggs from the skillet.

Makes 4 servings.

(It's nice to serve Buttery Top Whole Wheat Raisin Bread [page 106] or Two Grain Bread [page 103] toast with these eggs.)

Buckwheat Waffles

<table>
<tr><td>INGREDIENTS</td><td>UTENSILS</td></tr>
<tr><td>

1 cup buckwheat flour
½ cup whole wheat or un-bleached enriched white flour
¼ teaspoon sea salt or iodized salt
1 teaspoon baking soda
1 teaspoon baking powder
1¼ cups buttermilk
2 eggs
5 tablespoons safflower, soy, or corn oil

</td><td>

measuring cups
measuring spoons
flour sifter
bowl
cooking spoon
waffle iron

</td></tr>
</table>

Sift together flours, salt, baking soda, and baking powder into a bowl. Shake up a container of buttermilk and add 1¼ cups buttermilk to the flour mixture, along with eggs and oil. Mix well. If batter is not thin enough to pour easily, add 1 or 2 tablespoons of water.

Ask an adult to show you how your waffle iron works. Then bake waffles. Serve hot with Honey Bee Butter (page 43), soft margarine, maple syrup, or molasses.

Makes 4 to 6 waffles.

Honey Bee Butter

INGREDIENTS

2 tablespoons safflower, soy, or corn oil soft margarine
¼ cup honey
2 tablespoons orange juice
pinch of sea salt or iodized salt
1 egg white (see how to separate an egg, page 32)

UTENSILS

measuring spoons
small saucepan
cooking spoon
electric mixer (see page 24)

Melt margarine in a small saucepan over low heat. Set aside.

Combine honey, orange juice, salt, and egg white in small bowl of electric mixer and beat at high speed for about 10 minutes until mixture thickens. Add melted butter and stir in with a spoon.

Spread on waffles, pancakes, toast, bread, or muffins. Use it the same day you make it.

Super Wheat Hot Cereal

INGREDIENTS

¼ cup uncooked wheat
   cereal such as Wheatena
generous pinch of sea salt
   or iodized salt
⅓ cup raisins
2 cups cold water
¼ cup unsalted cashew
   nuts
2 tablespoons honey

UTENSILS

saucepan
measuring cups
measuring spoons
cooking spoon
chef's knife

Mix together in a saucepan the wheat cereal, salt, raisins, and water. Bring to boil, reduce heat, and simmer 5 to 8 minutes, stirring occasionally, until cereal gets as thick as you like it. While cereal is cooking chop the nuts. Remove cereal from stove and stir in nuts and honey. Spoon into 2 cereal bowls. Serve with milk.

Makes 2 servings.

LUNCH DISHES

Crunchburgers

INGREDIENTS

1 pound ground beef
¼ cup chopped water
chestnuts
2 tablespoons hulled
sunflower seeds
(kernels)
¼ teaspoon ground ginger
1 tablespoon soy sauce
dash of pepper
1 tablespoon peanut oil

UTENSILS

chef's knife
bowl
measuring cups
measuring spoons
cooking spoon
skillet
pancake turner

Chop water chestnuts. Place in a bowl with ground beef, sunflower seeds, ginger, soy sauce, and pepper; mix together with your hands. Shape into 6 hamburgers.

Put oil in skillet and heat over medium high heat. Arrange crunchburgers in skillet without crowding them. Brown on one side (3 to 5 minutes), turn with pancake turner, and brown other side. If you like them well done they will take a minute or two longer. Serve one on each plate.

Makes 6 servings.

Super Peanut Butter

INGREDIENTS

*1½ cups shelled peanuts,
either roasted or dry
roasted*
¼ cup wheat germ
*1 tablespoon turbinado
sugar or firmly packed
brown sugar*
*2 tablespoons safflower,
soy, or corn oil (for a
stronger flavor you can
use sesame oil instead)*

UTENSILS

measuring cups
measuring spoons
meat grinder (see page 25)
bowl
cooking spoon
*1-pint glass jar with tight
lid*

Put peanuts through a meat grinder with a medium-sized blade, letting ground peanuts drop into a bowl. Add wheat germ, sugar, and oil, and mix. Put mixture through meat grinder again, this time with a fine blade.

Make yourself a peanut butter sandwich, or spread some on crackers. Put the excess peanut butter in a glass jar until you're ready to use it again.

Tuna Toss Sandwich

INGREDIENTS

1 6½-ounce can tuna fish
3 tablespoons safflower,
 soy, or regular mayon-
 naise
¼ cup chopped celery
1 tablespoon lemon juice
1 tablespoon capers,
 drained
dash of pepper
4 slices Two Grain Bread
 (see page 103) or other
 bread

UTENSILS

bowl
cooking spoon
chef's knife
measuring spoons
measuring cup
juice squeezer
table knife

Chop the celery. Squeeze the lemon juice. Combine all ingredients except bread in a bowl. Spread on 2 slices of bread, cover with remaining 2 slices, and cut sandwiches in half.

Makes 2 sandwiches.

Vegetable Alphabet Soup

INGREDIENTS	UTENSILS
2 *tablespoons safflower, soy, or corn oil*	*vegetable peeler*
1 cup chopped onions	*paring knife*
1 cup chopped carrots	*chef's knife*
1 cup sliced celery	*cutting board*
1 cup sliced green beans	*vegetable brush*
½ cup peas (fresh or frozen)	*measuring cups*
1 cup chopped tomatoes	*measuring spoons*
2 tablespoons chopped fresh parsley	*large pot*
2 cups coarsely chopped cabbage	*cooking spoon*
4 cups beef broth	
few dashes of pepper	
1 bay leaf	
¼ cup enriched alphabet noodles	

Wash carrots, celery, green beans, tomatoes, parsley, and cabbage. Peel and chop onion. Chop carrots, and slice celery. Slice green beans, and chop tomatoes, discarding stem part. Cut cabbage in quarters, cut out core and discard, and chop cabbage coarsely. (Save any extra cabbage to make Pineapple Cabbage, page 87.)

Heat oil in a large pot and add onions, carrots, and celery. Sauté until lightly browned, stirring occasionally.

Add beef broth, green beans, peas, tomatoes, cabbage, parsley, bay leaf, and pepper. Bring to boil, cover, reduce heat, and simmer 30 minutes. Taste soup and add a little salt if you think it needs some. Add alphabet noodles and cook 10 minutes longer. Serve very hot.

Makes 8 servings.

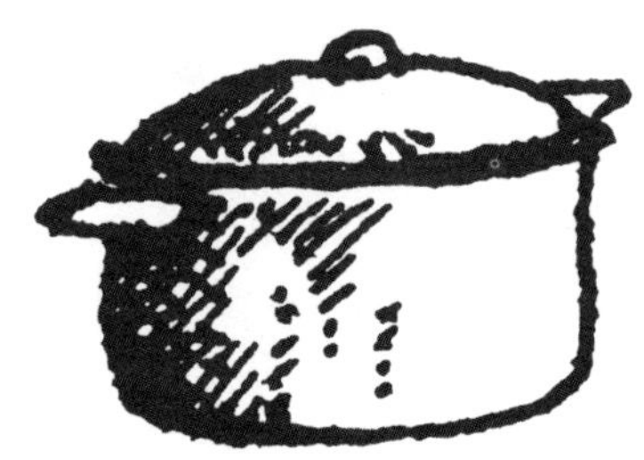

Big Baked Stuffed Shells

INGREDIENTS FOR SHELLS

1 12-ounce box jumbo
   macaroni shells
1 tablespoon sea salt or
   iodized salt
1 10-ounce package frozen
   chopped spinach,
   thawed
1 8-ounce container
   ricotta cheese or small
   curd cottage cheese
4 ounces mozzarella
   cheese, coarsely shredded
1 egg
1 teaspoon basil
1 teaspoon oregano
generous pinch of nutmeg
¼ teaspoon sea salt or
   iodized salt
dash of pepper

INGREDIENTS FOR

SAUCE
2 tablespoons safflower,
   soy, or corn oil soft
   margarine
2 tablespoons whole wheat
   flour
1 cup milk
½ cup chicken broth

UTENSILS

baking dish, about 8 by 12
   inches
shredder/grater (see page
   26)
wire whisk
small bowl
cooking spoons
measuring spoons
strainer
bowl
measuring cups
large pot
long-handled wooden
   spoon
slotted spoon
colander
small saucepan

*¼ teaspoon sea salt or
    iodized salt*
dash of pepper
pinch of nutmeg
*6 tablespoons grated
    Parmesan cheese*

Grease baking dish. Shred the mozzarella. Beat the egg lightly in a small bowl. Grate the Parmesan cheese. If you are using cottage cheese instead of ricotta, rub it through a fine strainer using the back of a spoon.

Place half of the thawed spinach in a strainer and press it with the back of a spoon to remove any excess water. Put the other half away for another use. Put the drained spinach in a bowl. Add the ricotta or cottage cheese and mozzarella, and mix. Add the beaten egg, basil, oregano, nutmeg, ¼ teaspoon salt, and pepper, and mix thoroughly.

Put 4 quarts cold water in a large pot and bring to boil. Add 1 tablespoon salt. Count out 24 shells and drop them into the pot. Boil for 9 minutes, stirring occasionally with a long-handled wooden spoon. Scoop out shells with a slotted spoon and put them in a colander. Rinse under cold water and allow them to drain for a minute. Put a heaping tablespoonful of cheese-spinach filling into each shell. As you fill the shells, arrange them side by side in baking dish in a single layer with the filling side up.

Turn on oven to heat at 350°. Melt the margarine in a small saucepan over medium flame. Stir in the flour and cook for 1 minute, stirring constantly. Add the milk and stir with a wire whisk until mixture thickens. Add the chicken broth, ¼ teaspoon salt, pepper, and nutmeg, and cook, stirring constantly, about 5 minutes. Remove from stove and stir in ¼ cup grated Parmesan. Spoon the sauce evenly over the shells in the baking dish. Sprinkle with the remaining grated Parmesan. Place in oven and bake 30 minutes.

Makes 6 servings (4 shells per serving).

Eggplant-Bottom Pizzas

INGREDIENTS	UTENSILS
1 small eggplant	*paper towel*
½ cup tomato sauce	*chef's knife*
2 tablespoons coarsely	*cookie sheet*
grated onion	*measuring cups*
2 teaspoons oregano	*measuring spoons*
sea salt or iodized salt	*shredder/grater (see page*
pepper	*26)*
¾ cup coarsely grated	*bowl*
mozzarella, Monterey	*cooking spoon*
Jack, or muenster cheese	*pancake turner*

Turn on oven to heat at 350°. Grate the cheese and onion.

Wash eggplant and dry it with paper towel. Cut 6 eggplant slices about ¼ inch thick. Lay the slices on a cookie sheet. (Save the rest of the eggplant, wrapped in plastic wrap, to make more of this recipe later. The eggplant can be stored for 2 or 3 days.)

In a bowl combine tomato sauce, grated onion, and oregano. Spoon mixture over eggplant slices. Sprinkle a little salt and pepper over each slice. Sprinkle 2 tablespoons grated cheese over each slice.

Place cookie sheet in oven and bake 15–20 minutes until cheese is melted and nicely browned. Remove from oven and, with pancake turner, put 2 eggplant slices on each plate. Eat with knives and forks.

Makes 3 servings.

Hint: If you want to you can put an anchovy or pieces of sautéed mushrooms on each pizza before you sprinkle on the cheese. To sauté mushrooms wash and slice 2 large mushrooms and sauté in 1 or 2 tablespoons soft margarine in a skillet. (You might want to serve Crybaby Cucumbers, page 84, with the pizzas.)

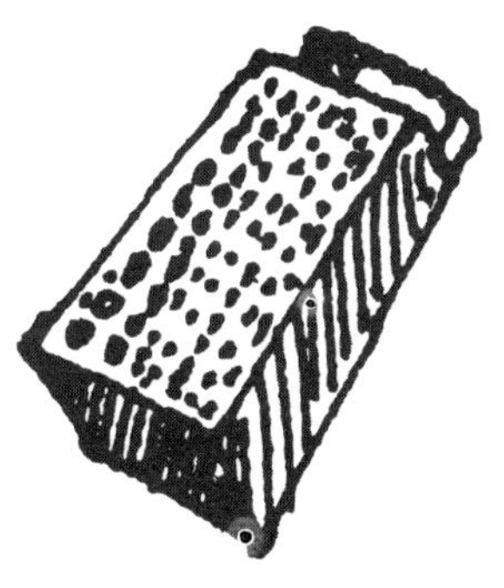

Fresh Tomato Soup with Cheese Stars

INGREDIENTS FOR

SOUP

2½ cups chopped tomatoes
   (3 to 5 ripe tomatoes)
¼ cup safflower, soy, or
   corn oil soft margarine
1 small chopped onion
2 tablespoons whole wheat
   flour
2½ cups milk
½ teaspoon sea salt or
   iodized salt
½ teaspoon basil
dash of pepper

UTENSILS

FOR SOUP

chef's knife
measuring cups
measuring spoons
cooking spoon
saucepan
electric blender (see page
   23)

INGREDIENTS

FOR CHEESE STARS

4 slices whole wheat bread
   or Two Grain Bread
   (page 103)
slices of Cheddar cheese or
American cheese

UTENSILS

FOR CHEESE STARS

toaster
star-shaped cookie cutter
cookie sheet
spatula or pancake turner

Wash and chop enough tomatoes to make 2½ cups, discarding stem ends. Place in saucepan with margarine. Chop onion and add to saucepan. Cover and simmer over low flame 15 minutes, stirring several times.

If you want to serve Cheese Stars with the soup, start to make them while the soup is simmering. Toast the bread. With cookie cutter cut out as many stars as you can from the toast slices. (Save leftover toast to make bread crumbs for another recipe.) Cut out the same number of stars from cheese slices. Place toast stars on cookie sheet. Place cheese stars on top of toast stars. Set aside.

Ask an adult to show you how to use your electric blender. Remove soup from stove and pour into blender. Cover blender. Blend at low speed for 10 seconds. Turn off blender. Remove cover and add flour. Put cover back on and blend 5 more seconds. Remove cover and pour soup back into saucepan. Stir in milk, salt, basil, and pepper. Heat just to boiling, lower flame, cover and simmer 5 minutes.

If you're making Cheese Stars turn on broiler so it heats while soup is simmering. After broiler has heated 2 minutes, place the cookie sheet under broiler for a minute or two until cheese melts and is bubbly. Watch carefully all the while so the cheese will not burn. Remove cookie sheet from oven and use a spatula or pancake turner to remove stars and place on a serving plate.

If the soup is ready before you've finished making the Cheese Stars, just turn off the flame under the soup and leave the saucepan covered until you're ready to serve it.

Pour soup into bowls.

Makes 4 servings.

Falafel (*Chick Pea Croquettes*)

<table>
<tr><td valign="top" width="50%">

INGREDIENTS

*1½ cups cooked chick peas
(garbanzos) (see page
30), or 1 15- or
16-ounce can chick
peas, drained*
1 or 2 cloves garlic
*2 tablespoons fine dry
bread crumbs, prefera-
bly whole wheat*
1 egg
*2 tablespoons chopped
fresh parsley*
*¼ teaspoon sea salt or
iodized salt*
½ teaspoon cumin
*¼ teaspoon ground
coriander (optional)*
dash of pepper
*dash of cayenne (use more
if you like spicy food)*
*safflower, soy, or corn oil
for frying*

</td><td valign="top" width="50%">

UTENSILS

*chef's knife or paring
knife*
measuring spoons
garlic press (optional)
food mill or strainer
measuring cup
cooking spoons
bowl
small bowl
wire whisk or egg beater
plate
ruler
10-inch skillet
pancake turner
paper towels

</td></tr>
</table>

Chop the parsley. Chop garlic very finely or put it through a garlic press. Put cooked chick peas through a food mill or force through a strainer using the back of a spoon to rub them through into a bowl.

Add garlic and bread crumbs to the chick peas and mix. Beat the egg lightly in a small bowl and add it to the chick peas, mixing well. Add the parsley, salt, cumin, coriander, pepper, and cayenne, and mix well. Divide the mixture into 16 equal parts. Form each part into a ball with your hands. Flatten each ball to ½ inch thick. Set on a plate.

Pour enough oil into a skillet so that it is ¼ inch deep. Place over medium flame and heat until oil is hot but not smoking. Put 8 falafel in skillet with a pancake turner. Fry on one side until nicely browned, about 3 minutes. Turn with pancake turner and brown on the other side 2 or 3 minutes. Remove with pancake turner and drain on paper towels. Fry the remaining falafel and drain on paper towels.

Serve on plates or use to make Falafel in Pita Bread (page 60).

Makes 4 servings (16 falafel).

Falafel in Pita Bread

INGREDIENTS	UTENSILS
16 Falafel (page 58)	*small sharp knife*
4 pita bread, preferably	*chef's knife*
whole wheat	*spoon*
2 or 3 tomatoes, sliced	
shredded iceberg lettuce	
Tahini Dressing (page 94)	

With a sharp knife, slit each pita bread open about ⅓ of the way around the edge. Slice tomatoes. Shred lettuce by cutting thin slices from the head of lettuce and pulling the slices into shreds.

Put 4 falafel in a pita bread. Put in 2 or 3 tomato slices. Put some shredded lettuce on the tomatoes. Spoon in some dressing. Prepare the 3 other pita bread in the same way.

Eat like sandwiches.

Makes 4 servings.

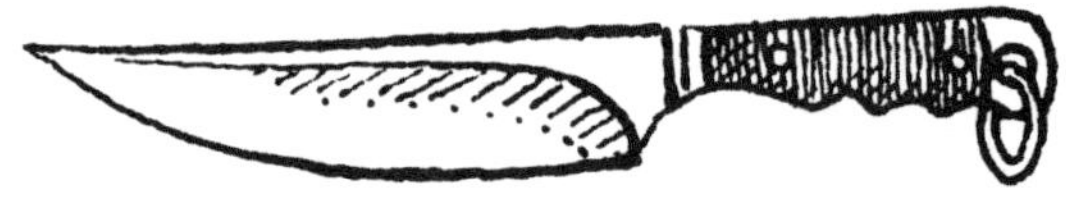

Sardine-Stuffed Hard-Cooked Eggs

INGREDIENTS

4 *eggs*
*¼ cup safflower or regular
   mayonnaise*
*1 can sardines, about 3¾
   ounces*
*2 tablespoons chopped
   black olives or green
   pimiento-stuffed olives*
*1 tablespoon finely chop-
   ped fresh parsley*
dash of pepper

UTENSILS

saucepan
measuring cup
measuring spoons
cooking spoons
paper towels
*paring knife or chef's
   knife*
2 shallow soup plates
sharp-tined fork

Let eggs stand at room temperature 30 minutes to 1 hour. Put 1 quart water in saucepan and bring to boil over high flame. Turn flame to medium low and lower the eggs, one at a time, into the water, using a long-handled spoon. Simmer them gently for 12 minutes. Remove pan from stove and set in sink under cold running water. Allow water to run for several minutes until eggs are cold. Crack each egg gently on table top and roll back and forth using a little pressure to crack the shell all around. Peel off the shells under cold running water. Pat the eggs dry on paper towels.

While eggs are simmering, chop the olives and the parsley.

Cut eggs in half lengthwise. Carefully remove the yolks and place them in a shallow soup plate. Mash the yolks with a sharp-tined fork. Add mayonnaise to yolks and mix thoroughly.

Drain the sardines, discarding the oil in which they are packed. Put the sardines on paper towels and pat them well to remove oil. Put half of them in a shallow soup plate and mash with sharp-tined fork. Put the other half away for another use.

Add mashed sardines to egg yolks and mix well. Add the olives, parsley, and pepper, and mix again. Divide the yolk mixture into 8 equal parts and spoon one part into each egg white. Place the stuffed eggs on a plate. Cover and chill 30 minutes or longer.

Makes 4 servings.

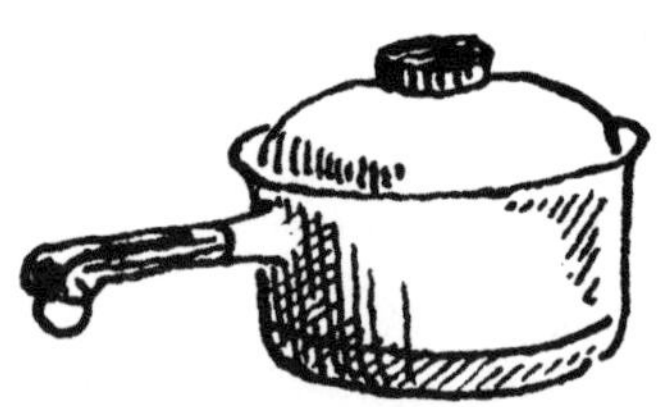

Mushroom Barley Soup

<table>
<tr><td>INGREDIENTS</td><td>UTENSILS</td></tr>
<tr><td>⅓ cup barley</td><td>strainer</td></tr>
<tr><td>3 cups beef broth</td><td>bowl</td></tr>
<tr><td>½ ounce dried mushrooms</td><td>measuring cups</td></tr>
<tr><td>1½ cups hot water</td><td>small bowl</td></tr>
<tr><td>1 tablespoon safflower,</td><td>saucepan</td></tr>
<tr><td> soy, or corn oil soft</td><td>strainer</td></tr>
<tr><td> margarine</td><td>measuring spoons</td></tr>
<tr><td>1½ cups milk</td><td>cooking spoon</td></tr>
</table>

Rinse barley in a strainer under cold running water. Combine barley and beef broth in a bowl and allow to stand for 2 hours. Pour barley and beef broth into saucepan and bring to a boil. Reduce heat, cover, and simmer 45 minutes.

While the barley is simmering, place the mushrooms in a small bowl and pour the hot water over them. Let them stand. After 45 minutes drain the mushrooms in a strainer and add them to the saucepan along with margarine and milk. Heat the soup, stirring, until it begins to simmer again. Partially cover the saucepan and simmer 15 minutes more, stirring occasionally.

Pour soup into cups or bowls.

Makes 4 to 6 servings.

SUPPER DISHES

Garden Casserole

INGREDIENTS

¾ cup elbow macaroni

1 teaspoon sea salt or iodized salt

2 tablespoons safflower, soy, or corn oil soft margarine

2 tablespoons safflower, soy, or corn oil

1 cup chopped onions

1 medium green pepper, cut into 1-inch squares (see page 31)

¼ pound mushrooms, sliced

1 large or 2 small tomatoes

¾ pound small zucchini, cut into ¾-inch slices

1½ cups cooked red kidney beans (see page 30), or 1 1-pound can red kidney beans, drained

2 tablespoons whole wheat flour

1½ cups chicken broth

1 teaspoon oregano

¼ teaspoon thyme

1 bay leaf

2 tablespoons wheat germ

¼ cup thinly sliced almonds

UTENSILS

covered casserole, 2½- to 3-quart size

large saucepan

measuring cups

measuring spoons

cooking spoons

slotted spoon

colander

chef's knife

paring knife

skillet

pancake turner

bowl

wooden spoon

wire whisk

table knife

Grease casserole. Put 2 quarts cold water in a large saucepan and bring to boil. Pour in salt. Sprinkle macaroni into boiling water and let it boil for 10 minutes, stirring every few minutes to make sure macaroni doesn't stick together or stick to the bottom of the pot. When macaroni has cooked for 10 minutes turn off stove. Scoop out macaroni with a slotted spoon and put into a colander. Rinse under cold water and allow to drain.

Turn on oven to heat at 350°. Chop the onions. Cut the green pepper into squares. Slice the mushrooms. Remove the cores from the tomatoes and cut them into 1-inch cubes. Trim the ends off the zucchini and slice them.

Place 1 tablespoon margarine and 1 tablespoon oil in skillet and set on medium flame. When margarine melts put the onions and green peppers in the skillet and sauté until lightly browned, turning them with pancake turner. Remove the onions and green peppers with a slotted spoon and put them in a bowl. Put the mushrooms in the skillet and sauté until lightly browned. Add them to the onions and peppers. Add 1 tablespoon oil to the skillet. Sprinkle the flour into the skillet and stir for a minute with a wooden spoon. Add the chicken broth and stir with a wire whisk until the mixture comes to a boil and is slightly thickened. Add the oregano, thyme, and bay leaf, and cook another minute, stirring. Remove skillet from stove.

Add the tomatoes, zucchini, kidney beans, and maca-roni to the onion mixture in the bowl and mix gently. Pour the chicken broth mixture into the bowl and mix again. Pour the mixture into the casserole and smooth down with the back of a spoon. Sprinkle wheat germ and sliced almonds over the top. Take 1 tablespoon margarine and use a table knife to put little pieces of it here and there over the top. Cover the casserole and bake in the oven for 20 minutes. Remove the cover and bake another 20 minutes.

Makes 6 to 8 servings.

(Crybaby Cucumbers, page 84, and some good crusty bread are nice with this casserole.)

Pork and Noodle Bake

INGREDIENTS FOR

CASSEROLE

*½ pound (8 ounces) en-
riched noodles, soy noo-
dles, or artichoke noo-
dles*
*1 tablespoon sea salt or
iodized salt*
2 tablespoons vegetable oil
½ cup chopped onion
1 pound ground pork
½ cup wheat germ
*1 8-ounce can tomato
sauce*
*2 tablespoons caraway
seeds*
1 teaspoon paprika
*¼ teaspoon sea salt or
iodized salt*
*1 tablespoon chopped fresh
parsley*
dash of pepper
pinch of sage

INGREDIENTS FOR

TOPPING

2 eggs
*⅓ cup milk or evaporated
milk*
*1½ tablespoons sesame
seeds*
*½ cup coarsely grated
Swiss cheese*
1 tablespoon wheat germ

UTENSILS

large pot
measuring spoons
measuring cups
strainer
colander
cooking spoons
chef's knife
skillet
*casserole, 2- to 2½-quart
size*
rubber spatula
small bowl
egg beater or whisk
*shredder/grater (see page
26)*

Put 4 quarts cold water in large pot and bring to a boil. Pour in 1 tablespoon salt. Sprinkle in the noodles and let them boil 7 to 8 minutes, stirring now and then with a spoon or fork to keep them separated. Turn off stove. Scoop out noodles with a strainer and put them in a colander. Rinse under cold water very well. Set aside.

Chop onions. Chop parsley. In skillet heat vegetable oil over medium flame and add onions. Cook until slightly browned. Break up ground pork into small pieces and add to onions. Cook, stirring and breaking up pork, until pork has just lost all its red color. Don't let it get brown or crusty. Remove skillet from stove. Stir in wheat germ, tomato sauce, caraway seeds, paprika, ¼ teaspoon salt, parsley, pepper, and sage. Mix well.

Turn on oven to heat at 350°. Grease casserole and put one-third of the noodles in the bottom. Then spoon half the pork mixture on the noodles and spread out evenly with rubber spatula. Put another third of the noodles over the pork. Then put the rest of the pork on the noodles and spread evenly. Put on the rest of the noodles.

Topping: Grate the Swiss cheese. In a small bowl beat eggs. Stir in milk, sesame seeds, and cheese. Pour evenly over top of noodles. Sprinkle 1 tablespoon wheat germ over top. Bake 45 minutes.

Makes 6 servings.

(Pineapple Cabbage, page 87, is good with this casse-role.)

Turkey Drumsticks in Orange Sauce

INGREDIENTS

*2 turkey drumsticks
weighing about 1½
pounds each
4 or 5 tablespoons whole
wheat flour
2 or 3 tablespoons olive oil
1 cup chopped onion
1 clove garlic, finely chopped
½ cup orange juice
grated rind of 1 orange
¼ cup sherry wine
¼ teaspoon cinnamon
½ cup chicken broth
3 tablespoons water*

UTENSILS

*chef's knife
paring knife
shredder/grater (see page
26)
orange squeezer
measuring cups
measuring spoons
paper towels
oval or round top-of-stove
casserole, 4- or 5-quart
size
big fork
plate
wooden spoon
wooden carving board
carving knife
fork
serving platter
aluminum foil
cup
cooking spoon*

Chop the onions. Chop the garlic finely. Grate the orange rind. Squeeze the orange juice.

Wash drumsticks under cold running water and pat dry with paper towels. Rub all over with 2 or 3 table- spoons of flour. Pour 2 tablespoons oil into casserole and place on stove. Turn on heat to medium high. When oil has heated for a few seconds put the drum- sticks in the casserole and brown them on all sides, turning them with a big fork as they brown. Add more oil if the casserole gets dry. Remove the drumsticks with the fork and set them on a plate.

Lower the flame to medium. Add the onions to the casserole and cook until very soft, stirring with wooden spoon. Add the garlic and stir. Put the drumsticks back in the casserole. Add orange juice, orange rind, sherry wine, cinnamon, and chicken broth. Stir, and bring to boil. Lower flame. Cover casserole. Simmer gently for 45 minutes. Remove the cover and turn the drumsticks over. Put the cover back on and simmer another 45 minutes.

Remove the drumsticks from casserole and place on a wooden carving board. Slice meat off drumsticks with carving knife, holding the drumstick steady with a fork. Discard bones and tendons. (Tendons look like long, thin, flat bones.) Arrange the slices on serving platter. Cover with aluminum foil.

Mix 2 tablespoons flour and the water together in a cup. Add it to the casserole, stirring constantly. Cook until sauce thickens, and simmer another few minutes, stirring all the while. Spoon the sauce over the turkey slices and serve.

Makes 4 servings.

(Honey Corn, page 89, is especially good with these turkey drumsticks.)

Beefy Baked Beans

INGREDIENTS	UTENSILS
1 pound dried navy beans (pea beans)	*strainer*
cold water	*large bowl*
½ cup unsulphured molasses	*large pot*
½ cup chili sauce (homemade or a brand without artificial flavoring)	*chef's knife*
½ teaspoon ginger	*slotted spoon*
dash of pepper	*bean pot or tall narrow covered casserole, 2- to 2½-quart size*
1 large onion	*measuring cups*
¼ pound beef chuck	*measuring spoons*
½ cup or more beef broth	*cooking spoon*

Sort out the beans and discard any withered or darkened ones and any stones or other material you may find with the beans. Wash beans in a strainer under cold running water. Place beans in a large bowl. Pour enough cold water over them to cover them by 2½ inches. Allow beans to soak overnight, or about 12 hours.

Transfer the beans and water to a large pot and bring to a boil. Lower flame and let the beans simmer gently for 45 minutes. Turn off stove.

Preheat oven at 300°. Remove beans from pot with a slotted spoon and put into bean pot. Add molasses, chili sauce, ginger, and pepper, and mix gently. Peel the onion and cut it into quarters. Using a cooking spoon to move the beans, bury the piece of beef and the onion pieces in the beans. Pour enough beef broth over the beans until it just covers them.

Cover bean pot and place it in oven. Bake 4 hours. Once each hour remove the lid and stir the beans by spooning them gently from the bottom of the pot to the top so that they cook evenly. Push the onions back down if they come to the top. Each time add enough beef broth so that it just covers the beans. If you run out of beef broth, use the bean cooking water.

At the end of 4 hours stir the beans again and add beef broth if necessary. Bake 30 minutes longer without the lid. Serve each person some of the beef with the beans.

Makes 6 servings.

(Crunchy Salad, page 92, goes nicely with Beefy Baked Beans.)

Flounder on Spinach Bed with Cheese Blanket

INGREDIENTS

2 10-ounce packages fro-
zen chopped spinach
½ cup boiling water
1 cup sour cream
1 tablespoon whole wheat
or unbleached enriched
white flour
¼ teaspoon sea salt or
iodized salt
¼ teaspoon nutmeg
dash of pepper
1 pound flounder fillets
(either fresh or frozen
and thawed)
2 tablespoons safflower,
soy, or corn oil soft
margarine
⅛ teaspoon sea salt or
iodized salt
1½ teaspoons paprika
¼ cup grated Parmesan or
Swiss cheese

UTENSILS

2 saucepans
measuring cups
measuring spoons
cooking spoon
cooking fork
colander
bowl
shallow casserole, about 9
inches square or similar
size
paper towels
pastry brush
shredder/grater (see page
26)

Put spinach in a saucepan and pour boiling water over it. Cover and bring to a boil. Uncover, lower heat, and allow to simmer, separating the spinach with a big fork until it is completely thawed. Drain spinach in a colander and place in a bowl.

Turn on oven to heat at 375°. Grease casserole. Grate cheese.

Add sour cream, flour, ¼ teaspoon salt, nutmeg, and pepper to the spinach and mix well. Spoon into casserole.

Rinse flounder fillets under cold running water. Pat them dry with paper towels and arrange on top of spinach in a single layer.

Melt margarine in small saucepan over low heat. Brush fillets with the melted margarine. Sprinkle with ⅛ teaspoon salt and 1½ teaspoons paprika. Sprinkle grated cheese over fillets. Place in oven and bake 25 minutes.

Makes 4 servings.

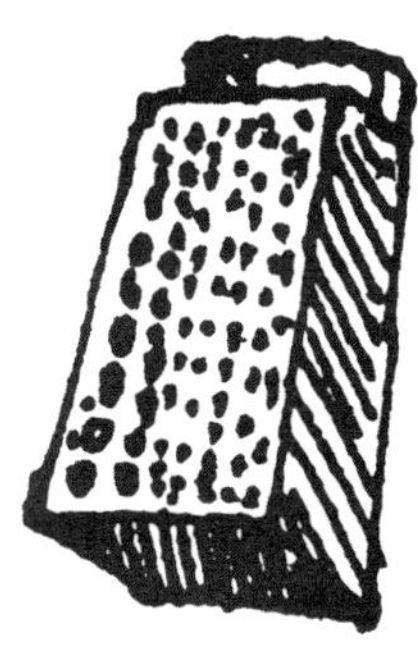

Chili Chicken

<table>
<tr><td>INGREDIENTS</td><td>UTENSILS</td></tr>
<tr><td>1 broiling chicken cut into quarters</td><td>paper towels</td></tr>
<tr><td>2 tablespoons chili powder</td><td>shallow glass or china baking dish</td></tr>
<tr><td>1 tablespoon oregano</td><td>small bowl</td></tr>
<tr><td>1 teaspoon sea salt or iodized salt</td><td>measuring cup</td></tr>
<tr><td>¼ teaspoon pepper</td><td>measuring spoons</td></tr>
<tr><td>½ cup safflower, soy, or corn oil</td><td>brush or rubber spatula</td></tr>
<tr><td></td><td>plastic wrap</td></tr>
<tr><td></td><td>cooking fork</td></tr>
</table>

Start this recipe early in the day, or even the night before.

Rinse chicken under cold running water and pat dry with paper towels. Place in baking dish.

Mix together in a small bowl chili powder, oregano, salt, and pepper. Stir in oil and mix well. Pour this mixture over chicken pieces and rub in with brush or rubber spatula, or with your fingers, so that chicken is covered all over. Cover the baking dish with plastic wrap and set in refrigerator to marinate for 8 hours or longer, turning chicken pieces over once or twice during that time and re-covering with the plastic wrap each time.

Turn on broiler to heat. Place chicken pieces on broiler rack 6 inches from heat and broil 15 minutes on one side. Brush with the chili powder mixture once while broiling. Turn chicken over and broil another 15 minutes, brushing again with chili powder mixture. Test chicken with a fork, and if tender, it is ready to serve. If not done, turn again and cook another 10 minutes, brushing with chili powder mixture. Repeat every 10 minutes until done.

Makes 4 servings.

(Chili Chicken is nice with Rice Olé, page 98, and Lemon Broccoli, page 90.)

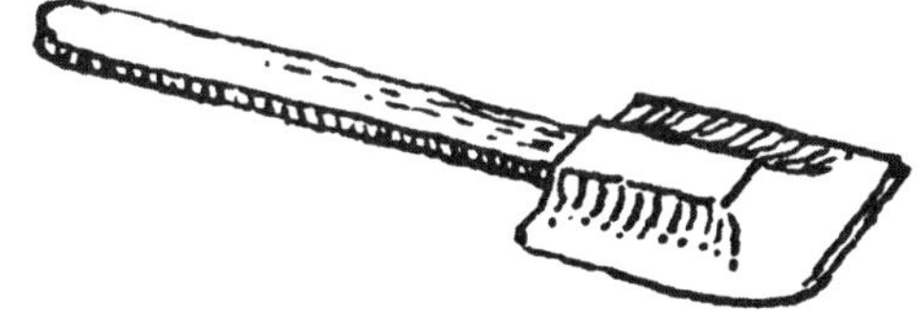

Baked Beef
in Herb-Tomato Sauce

INGREDIENTS

*1 tablespoon safflower,
  soy, or corn oil*
*2½-pound beef chuck
  roast*
¾ cup sliced onions
1 clove garlic
few dashes of pepper
½ teaspoon rosemary
*1 tablespoon chopped fresh
  parsley*
pinch of thyme
*1 8-ounce can tomato
  sauce*
½ cup beef broth
1 bay leaf
*¼ pound fresh mush-
  rooms, sliced (optional)*

UTENSILS

*heavy top-of-stove cas-
  serole or Dutch oven*
measuring cups
measuring spoons
cooking fork
chef's knife

Turn on oven to heat at 350°. Slice the onions. Chop garlic and parsley. Set aside.

Pour oil into casserole and place on stove over medium high heat. Brown chuck roast in oil, turning roast with a big fork until all sides are browned. Add more oil if it gets dry. Add onions, stirring so onions will brown. Add garlic and sprinkle meat with pepper, rosemary, parsley, and thyme. Pour tomato sauce and beef broth around the meat and drop in bay leaf.

Cover casserole and bake in oven for 1 hour and 15 minutes. (If you wish you can add ¼ pound fresh sliced mushrooms to the casserole after it has baked for 1 hour.) Remove cover and test with a big fork to see if roast is tender (see page 30). Bake 15 minutes longer if necessary. Discard bay leaf and remove roast from casserole. Put it on a large platter and cut into slices. Spoon the sauce over the sliced meat.

Makes 6 servings.

(Zippy Carrot Packs, page 88, can bake in the oven about 45 minutes after the beef goes into the oven if you'd like to serve them too.)

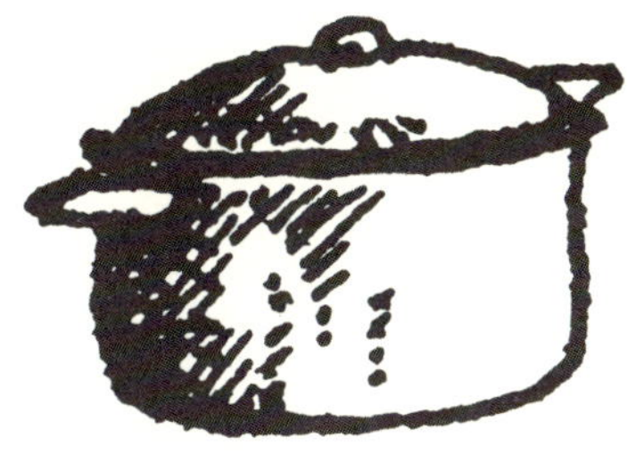

Sweet and Sour Tuna

INGREDIENTS
1 green pepper
1 medium-sized onion
1 tablespoon safflower,
  soy, or corn oil
2 6½-ounce cans tuna,
  drained
1 8-ounce can sliced un-
  sweetened pineapple
1 tablespoon cornstarch
1 tablespoon vinegar
2 teaspoons soy sauce
dash of pepper

UTENSILS
paring knife
chef's knife
measuring spoons
skillet
small bowl
cooking spoons

Cut green pepper into strips and chop onion. Heat oil in skillet over medium flame and sauté green pepper and onion until onion looks transparent. Stir in tuna, breaking up any large chunks.

Pour syrup from the canned pineapple into a bowl and stir in cornstarch. Add to the tuna, stirring gently until it thickens. Cut pineapple slices into quarters and add to the tuna. Stir in vinegar, soy sauce, and pepper. Cover and simmer over low flame until heated through, about 5 minutes.

Makes 4 servings

(This is good served with Buttery Brown Rice, page 91.)

VEGETABLES AND RICE

Crybaby Cucumbers

INGREDIENTS	UTENSILS
3 cucumbers	*chef's knife*
3–4 thin slices onion	*vegetable peeler*
1 teaspoon sea salt or	*bowl*
iodized salt	*measuring spoons*
½ cup sour cream	*measuring cup*
1 teaspoon dill weed	*cooking spoon*
2 tablespoons vinegar	*colander*
dash of pepper	

Wash, dry, and slice cucumbers very thinly. If the cucumbers have a waxy coating you'll have to peel them before slicing. Place cucumber slices in a bowl. Add onion slices and salt and let stand at room temperature for 1 hour. Liquid will come from the cucumbers while they stand.

At the end of 1 hour drain the cucumbers in a colander and throw away the "tears." Return cucumbers and onions to the bowl and add sour cream, dill weed, vinegar, and pepper. Chill half an hour before serving.

Makes 6 servings.

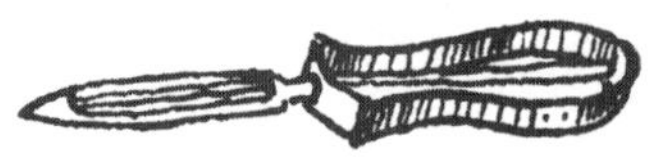

Lettuce and Tomato Tumble

<table>
<tr><td>

INGREDIENTS

*1 small head romaine or 1
large head Boston let-
tuce, or any garden let-
tuce you have*

*1 small basket cherry
tomatoes (you can add
any other raw vegeta-
bles you like, such as
carrot slices, broccoli
flowerettes, or spinach
leaves)*

</td><td>

UTENSILS

*big pan
colander
paper towels
salad bowl or plastic bag
paring knife
salad fork and spoon*

</td></tr>
</table>

Wash lettuce in a big pan of cold water by swishing the leaves up and down in the water. Drain leaves in a colander and dry them between paper towels. Tear into small pieces and place in salad bowl, or put in a plastic bag and store in refrigerator until ready to use.

Wash cherry tomatoes in cold water and dry with paper towels. Cut them in half and put them with the lettuce in salad bowl. Pour Shake-Up Dressing (page 86) over salad and toss with salad fork and spoon.

Makes 4 to 6 servings.

Shake-Up Dressing

INGREDIENTS
3 tablespoons safflower, soy, or corn oil
1 tablespoon vinegar
¼ teaspoon sea salt or iodized salt
dash of pepper
¼ teaspoon prepared mustard
¼ teaspoon basil

UTENSILS
measuring spoons
small glass jar with tight lid

Place all ingredients in jar. Close tightly with lid. Shake up dressing well. Pour over salad.

Pineapple Cabbage

<table>
<tr><td>INGREDIENTS</td><td>UTENSILS</td></tr>
<tr><td>1 cup unsweetened
  pineapple juice</td><td>measuring cup
saucepan</td></tr>
<tr><td>1 small cabbage</td><td>chef's knife</td></tr>
<tr><td>1 tablespoon safflower,
  soy, or corn oil soft
  margarine</td><td>cooking spoon
cooking fork
measuring spoons</td></tr>
</table>

Pour pineapple juice into a saucepan and heat for several minutes over low flame.

While pineapple juice is heating, wash cabbage and remove any wilted leaves. Cut in half and cut out core. Slice cabbage crosswise into ¼-inch slices. Place in the saucepan with the pineapple juice. Cover and simmer over low flame until cabbage is tender but still a little crisp. Test it with a fork. Add margarine and pour into serving bowl.

Makes 4 to 6 servings.

Zippy Carrot Packs

INGREDIENTS
1 pound small carrots
safflower, soy or corn oil
soft margarine
chopped pimiento
chili sauce
pepper

UTENSILS
6 pieces of aluminum foil,
each about 8 x 12 inches
paring knife
vegetable peeler
measuring spoons

Turn on oven to heat at 350°.

Wash carrots and scrape with paring knife or peel with vegetable peeler. Slice thinly into rounds. Divide the carrots and place them on the six pieces of foil.

On each pile of carrot slices put 1 teaspoon margarine, 1 teaspoon chopped pimiento, ½ teaspoon chili sauce, and a pinch of pepper.

Bring long ends of foil together over the carrots and fold edges over and down several times to make a tight seam. Then fold ends up and fold them over several times to make a leakproof package. Place carrot packages in oven and bake 15 minutes. Turn packages over and bake another 15 minutes.

Makes 6 servings.

Honey Corn

2 *tablespoons honey*
4 *ears corn*
safflower, soy, or corn oil
　soft margarine
sea salt or iodized salt
pepper

large pot
measuring spoons
cooking spoon
cooking fork or tongs
paper towels

Fill a large pot half full of cold water. Place on stove, cover, and bring to boil. While water is coming to boil, remove shucks and silk from the ears of corn and rinse corn.

Remove cover from pot and stir in honey. Gently drop the corn into boiling water, being careful not to splash yourself. Cook 4 minutes (Be sure *not* to put any salt in the water, because it will make the corn tough.) Lift the corn out of water with a big fork or tongs and drain on paper towels.

Serve with margarine, salt, and pepper.

Makes 4 servings.

Lemon Broccoli

<table>
<tr><td>INGREDIENTS</td><td>UTENSILS</td></tr>
<tr><td>1 bunch fresh broccoli or 2 10-ounce packages frozen broccoli</td><td>paring knife</td></tr>
<tr><td>2 tablespoons safflower, soy, or corn oil soft margarine</td><td>large saucepan
small saucepan
measuring spoons
juice squeezer</td></tr>
<tr><td>juice of 1 lemon</td><td>colander</td></tr>
<tr><td>dash of pepper</td><td></td></tr>
</table>

If using fresh broccoli, cut off any dry stem ends or bruised spots and pull off any wilted leaves. Wash and place broccoli in large saucepan. Pour in about a cup of boiling water, cover tightly, and cook over low flame until just tender, not soft, about 10 minutes. If using frozen broccoli, cook according to package directions until just tender.

While broccoli is cooking, squeeze the lemon, removing any seeds. Melt margarine in small saucepan over low heat. Add lemon juice and pepper.

Drain broccoli in colander and place in serving dish. Pour lemon butter over broccoli. Serve with salt and pepper.

Makes 6 servings.

Buttery Brown Rice

INGREDIENTS
2½ *cups cold water*
½ *teaspoon sea salt or*
  iodized salt
1 *cup brown rice*
3 *tablespoons safflower,*
  soy, or corn oil soft
  margarine

UTENSILS
measuring cups
measuring spoons
saucepan
cooking spoon
cooking fork

In saucepan combine water, salt, and brown rice. Bring to boil over high heat and boil 5 minutes. Reduce heat, cover, and simmer 45 minutes. Leave the cover on all the time—and don't peek.

Remove lid after 45 minutes, fluff rice with a fork, and stir in margarine. Don't worry if rice sticks to the bottom or scorches a little. It tastes good that way and some people like the bottom part best.

Makes 4 to 6 servings.

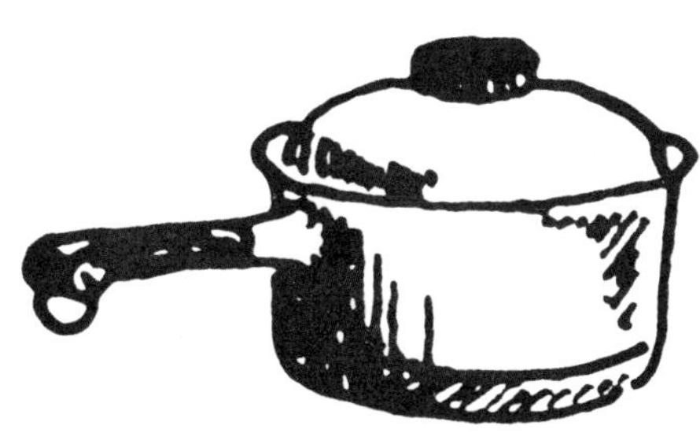

Crunchy Salad

INGREDIENTS

1 small head romaine let-
tuce
3 small- to medium-size
carrots
2 ribs celery
1 cup soy bean sprouts, al-
falfa sprouts, or mung
bean sprouts

UTENSILS

big pan
colander
paper towels
large plate or platter
vegetable brush
paring knife
strainer
bowl
measuring cup
cooking spoon
salad fork and spoon

Wash lettuce in a big pan of cold water by swishing the leaves up and down in the water. Drain leaves in a colander and dry them between paper towels. Tear into small pieces and arrange on a large plate or a platter. Place in refrigerator.

Wash the carrots with a vegetable brush. Cut the ends off them, and scrape them with a paring knife. Cut them in half lengthwise. Lay the halves down flat and cut them in half lengthwise. Then cut the carrot pieces crosswise into 2-inch strips. Put into a bowl.

Wash the celery with vegetable brush, and trim off the ends. Cut off the leaves and save them for an- other use. Cut the celery diagonally into ½-inch pieces. Put in bowl with carrots. Rinse sprouts in a strainer under cold running water. Put the sprouts in the bowl and toss the vegetables together. Spoon them into the lettuce platter so they look nice. Spoon Tahini Dressing (page 94) all over the salad. Serve with salad fork and spoon.

Makes 8 servings.

(You can spoon Shake-Up Dressing [page 86] over the salad instead of Tahini Dressing if you want to.)

Tahini Dressing

INGREDIENTS

1 small garlic clove (if you like garlic a lot, use 2 cloves)

¼ teaspoon sea salt or iodized salt

dash of pepper

dash of cayenne pepper

1 tablespoon sesame oil (if you don't have sesame, use safflower, soy, or corn oil)

½ cup lemon juice (about 4 lemons)

½ cup tahini (ground sesame seed)

1 tablespoon finely chopped fresh parsley

1 teaspoon basil

1 teaspoon marjoram or oregano

UTENSILS

paring knife or chef's knife

garlic press (optional)

small bowl

measuring spoons

small spoon

cooking spoon

lemon squeezer

measuring cups

covered glass jar

Chop the parsley. Squeeze lemon juice. Cut end off garlic and peel it. Cut into small pieces or put through a garlic press, and put in a small bowl. Add salt, pepper, and cayenne pepper to garlic and mash together against the inside of the bowl with the back of a small spoon. Add the oil and mix. Add the lemon juice and tahini gradually, adding a little of each at a time and mixing well. Add the parsley, basil, and marjoram or oregano, and mix again. Pour into a glass jar. Cover and chill in refrigerator 1 hour or longer.

Remove from refrigerator when ready to use. If the dressing is a little too thick, add cold water, 1 tablespoon at a time, mixing well each time, until it is as thin as you like salad dressing. Spoon over salad or into Falafel in Pita Bread (page 60). Store unused dressing in covered jar in refrigerator.

Makes 1 generous cup.

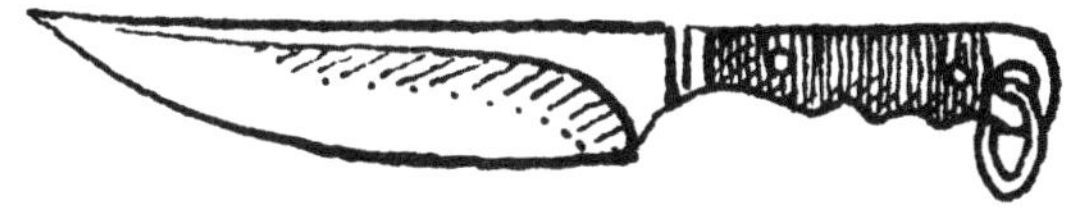

INGREDIENTS

1 large tart apple
*2 tablespoons safflower,
   soy, or corn oil soft
   margarine*
*½ cup light cream or
   half-and-half*
*dash of sea salt or iodized
   salt*
pinch of pepper
*1½ cups fresh lima beans
   or 1 10-ounce package
   frozen baby lima beans*
*1½ cups cut fresh green
   beans or 1 10-ounce
   package frozen cut
   green beans*

UTENSILS

2 saucepans
measuring cups
measuring spoons
cooking spoons
apple corer
chef's knife
colander

Wash apple and remove core (see page 32). Cut apple into cubes and place in small saucepan with margarine and cook until cubes are tender but still hold their shape. Add cream, salt, and pepper. Remove from flame and set aside.

Place lima beans in large saucepan and pour ½ cup boiling water over them. Bring to boil, lower flame, cover, and allow to simmer 20 minutes for fresh limas, or 5 minutes for frozen limas. Add green beans, bring to boil again, cover, and allow to simmer 6 minutes longer for fresh beans, or 3 minutes longer for frozen beans. Place a colander in the sink and drain the vegetables in the colander. Place vegetables back in saucepan and add the apple mixture. Stir gently and heat for 2 minutes over a low flame.

Makes 6 servings.

Rice Olé

INGREDIENTS	**UTENSILS**
1 tablespoon safflower, soy, or corn oil soft margarine	*chef's knife*
1 tablespoon safflower, soy, or corn oil	*paring knife*
1 cup brown rice	*skillet*
1 cup chopped onion	*cooking spoon*
1 large can Italian to-matoes (35-ounce size)	*measuring cups*
½ teaspoon sea salt or iodized salt	*measuring spoons*
few dashes of pepper	*aluminum foil*
1 teaspoon paprika	*casserole, about 2-quart size*
2 tablespoons chopped fresh parsley	*small fork*
pinch of saffron (if you have some on hand)	*shredder/grater (see page 26)*
¼ cup grated Parmesan or Romano cheese	
3 tablespoons sliced pimiento-stuffed olives	

Turn on oven to heat at 350°. Chop onions and parsley. Slice olives.

Put margarine and oil in skillet and melt over medium flame. Add brown rice and onions to skillet. Cook and stir until onion is soft. Add can of tomatoes, salt, pepper, paprika, parsley, and saffron. Mix well and spoon into greased casserole.

Cover with lid or aluminum foil and bake in oven for 1 hour. Grate the cheese. Look at the rice once during baking, and if it seems dry, stir in ¼ cup beef or chicken broth. After 1 hour remove lid and take some rice out with a fork. Let it cool and taste to see if it is tender. If not, bake 15 minutes longer. Remove from oven and stir in grated cheese and olives.

Makes 6 servings.

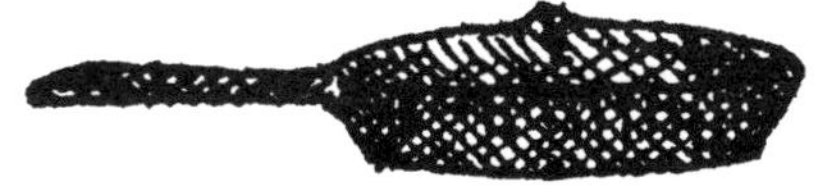

Roman Spinach

INGREDIENTS	UTENSILS
¼ cup raisins	small bowl
1 10-ounce bag fresh spinach	measuring cup
1 tablespoon safflower, soy, or corn oil	measuring spoons
	big pan
2 tablespoons pine nuts (pignolias)	colander
	saucepan
¼ teaspoon sea salt or iodized salt	cooking spoon
	strainer

Place raisins in a small bowl and pour enough boiling water over them to just cover. Set aside.

Plunge spinach into a big pan of cold water. Wash by swishing leaves up and down in the water. Place spinach in colander to drain. Remove any brown, yellow, or wilted leaves.

Put oil in a large saucepan and heat slightly. Add pine nuts, salt, and spinach and cover pan tightly. Lower flame and cook 3 to 5 minutes until spinach has wilted. Drain raisins in strainer and add to spinach. Toss well and serve.

Makes 3 servings.

BREADS

Pepita Pumpkin Bread

INGREDIENTS	UTENSILS
¾ cup honey	bowl
⅓ cup safflower, soy, or corn oil	cooking spoon
2 eggs	measuring cups
1 cup canned pumpkin	measuring spoons
1½ cups whole wheat flour	egg beater
½ teaspoon sea salt or iodized salt	flour sifter
½ teaspoon baking soda	loaf pan, about 9 x 5 inches
½ teaspoon baking powder	cake tester
1½ teaspoons cinnamon	wire rack
½ teaspoon nutmeg	
¼ teaspoon cloves	
½ cup shelled pumpkin seeds	

Turn on oven to heat at 325°. Grease loaf pan.

In a bowl mix together honey and oil. Add eggs and beat well with egg beater. Add pumpkin and stir well with a large spoon.

Sift together flour, salt, baking soda, baking powder, cinnamon, nutmeg, and cloves. Add to the pumpkin mixture and mix well. Add pumpkin seeds, mix, and pour into loaf pan.

Bake 1 hour or until cake tester inserted in center comes out clean. Remove from oven. Turn out on wire rack (see page 32) and allow to cool before slicing.

Two Grain Bread

<table>
<tr><td>

INGREDIENTS

½ cup milk
¼ cup safflower, soy, or
  corn oil
2 tablespoons unsul-
  phured molasses
1 egg
¼ cup warm water (about
  115°)
1 package or 1 tablespoon
  active dry yeast
1 tablespoon brown sugar
1 cup rolled oats
1½ cups or more whole
  wheat flour
1 cup unbleached enriched
  white flour
½ teaspoon sea salt or
  iodized salt
1 tablespoon rolled oats

</td><td>

UTENSILS

2 large bowls
measuring cups
measuring spoons
cooking spoons
2 small bowls
egg beater
rubber spatula
medium bowl
plastic wrap
pastry board
loaf pan, 8½ x 4½ inches
pastry brush
wire rack

</td></tr>
</table>

Combine milk, oil, and molasses thoroughly in a large bowl. Beat egg lightly in a small bowl. Add egg to milk mixture, scraping out the small bowl with rubber spatula.

Run water from the hot water faucet until it feels quite warm on the inside of your wrist, but is not hot enough to hurt you (about 115°). Measure the warm water and put it in a small bowl. Sprinkle yeast over it, add brown sugar, and stir until the yeast and sugar are thoroughly dissolved. Place the bowl in the warmest place you can find in the kitchen away from open doors and windows. Let the yeast mixture sit 5 to 10 minutes until it becomes a little foamy.

While you're waiting for the yeast mixture, toss the 1 cup oats, 1½ cups whole wheat flour, white flour, and salt together in a medium bowl. When the yeast mixture is ready, scrape it into the milk-egg mixture, using rubber spatula. Mix. Add the oatmeal-flour mixture, half at a time, and mix until thoroughly blended. Form into a ball.

Sprinkle a little whole wheat flour on a pastry board or wooden work-table top. Turn the dough out onto the flour and knead (see page 29) 10 minutes. Form it into a ball.

Grease a large bowl. Set the dough in the bowl and turn it over so that all sides are greased. Cover the bowl with plastic wrap so that no air can get in. Place the bowl in a warm place and let the dough rise until double in size (1 to 1½ hours, or longer if necessary). Grease loaf pan.

Punch the dough down with your fists. Sprinkle a little flour on the board and turn the dough out onto the flour. Knead for 1 minute. Then flatten dough out with your hands as much as you can. Roll up like a jelly roll, very tightly. Shape it into a loaf. Turn the ends under and pinch them closed. Brush top of bread lightly with a pastry brush dipped in water.

With your fingers sprinkle the 1 tablespoon oatmeal over the loaf. Cover the loaf pan loosely with the plastic wrap and put it in a warm place to rise again until double in size, about 45 minutes.

About 10 minutes before dough has finished rising turn on oven to heat at 350°. Remove plastic wrap and place bread pan in center of oven. Bake 40 to 45 minutes. Remove from oven and turn bread out of pan onto wire rack. Tap the bottom of the loaf. It will sound hollow if the bread is done, and you can cool it on wire rack (see page 32). If not done, put back in pan and bake another 5 minutes.

When cool, slice as you need it for sandwiches, toast, or snacks.

Buttery Top Whole Wheat Raisin Bread

INGREDIENTS

1½ cups warm water
(about 115°)
1½ packages or 1½ ta-
blespoons active dry
yeast
2 tablespoons honey
1½ tablespoons safflower,
soy, or corn oil
½ cup nonfat dry milk
powder
1 teaspoon sea salt or
iodized salt
4 to 5 cups whole wheat
flour
½ cup raisins
1 tablespoon whole wheat
flour
1 tablespoon safflower,
soy, or corn oil soft
margarine

UTENSILS

loaf pan, 9 x 5 inches
measuring cups
measuring spoons
large bowl
cooking spoons
custard cup
pastry board
wire rack
small saucepan
pastry brush

Turn on oven to heat at 150° or lowest setting. Grease loaf pan.

Run water from the hot water faucet until it feels quite warm on the inside of your wrist, but is not hot enough to hurt you (about 115°). Measure the warm water and put it in a large bowl. Sprinkle the yeast over the water, add honey, and stir until yeast is completely dissolved. Place bowl in the warmest place you can find in the kitchen away from open doors and windows. Let the yeast mixture sit 5 to 10 minutes until it becomes a little foamy. Add oil, dry milk powder, and salt. Add 4 cups flour, 2 cups at a time, and mix until thoroughly combined. In a custard cup mix the raisins with 1 tablespoon flour. Add to the dough and mix until the raisins are scattered through the dough. If dough is not stiff, add enough of the remaining 1 cup flour so that it is fairly stiff.

Sprinkle a little flour on a pastry board or wooden work-table top. Turn the dough out onto the flour and knead (see page 29) 10 minutes, sprinkling a little more flour on the board as needed. Flatten dough out with your hands as much as you can. Roll up like a jelly roll, very tightly. Shape into a loaf. Turn ends under and pinch them closed. Fit into loaf pan. Set in warmed oven for 15 minutes.

Remove from oven and set in warm place away from open doors and windows. Turn oven temperature to 350° and wait 5 minutes. Return loaf pan to oven and bake 50 to 55 minutes.

Remove from oven and turn bread out of pan onto a wire rack. Tap the bottom of the loaf. It will sound hollow if the bread is done, and you can cool it on wire rack (see page 32). If not done, put back in pan and bake another 5 minutes.

Melt the margarine in a small saucepan and brush the top of the bread with it using pastry brush. When cool, slice as you need it for sandwiches, toast, or snacks.

Nutty Date-Banana Bread

<table>
<tr><td>

INGREDIENTS

⅓ cup safflower, soy, or
   corn oil soft margarine
1 cup firmly packed brown
   sugar
2 eggs
2 ripe bananas
1¾ cups whole wheat
   flour
2 teaspoons baking pow-
   der
¼ teaspoon baking soda
¼ teaspoon sea salt or
   iodized salt
½ cup chopped nuts
½ cup chopped and pitted
   dates

</td><td>

UTENSILS

bowl
measuring cups
measuring spoons
cooking spoon
fork
flour sifter
chef's knife
loaf pan, about 9 x 5 in-
   ches
cake tester
wire rack

</td></tr>
</table>

Turn on oven to heat at 350°. Grease loaf pan. Chop nuts and dates.

Cream margarine in a bowl until soft. Add sugar a little at a time, stirring well each time. Add eggs and mix well. Mash enough bananas with a fork to make 1 cup and mix into the egg mixture.

Sift together the flour, baking powder, baking soda, and salt. Add to the banana batter and stir well. Add nuts and dates and stir into the batter. Pour batter into loaf pan. Bake in oven for 1 hour or until a cake tester inserted in center of bread comes out clean. Remove from oven. Turn out on wire rack (see page 32) and allow to cool before slicing.

DESSERTS

INGREDIENTS

1 pint strawberries
1 cup heavy cream
½ teaspoon vanilla extract
turbinado sugar or brown sugar

UTENSILS

colander
paring knife or little spoon
bowl
egg beater
measuring cup
measuring spoons
cooking spoon

Wash strawberries quickly in cold water and drain them in a colander. Remove the hulls (green stem ends) with a paring knife, or scoop them out with a little spoon. Cut the strawberries in half, or in quarters if they're very large.

Whip cream in a bowl with egg beater until it just begins to hold its shape, but do not let it get stiff. Stir in vanilla extract. Stir in the strawberries.

Spoon out into 4 soup plates. Sprinkle sugar over each serving. Serve with dessert spoons.

Makes 4 servings.

You can make this recipe with blueberries instead of strawberries if you want to. Just wash the blueberries and leave them whole.

Orange Treat for One

INGREDIENTS

*1 orange, peeled, seeded,
    and cut in slices*
⅓ cup seedless grapes
1 tablespoon honey
*1 tablespoon chopped wal-
    nuts*

UTENSILS

paring knife
dessert dish
measuring cup
measuring spoons

Cut orange slices in quarters and grapes in half and place in dessert dish. Stir in honey and walnuts.

Makes 1 serving.

Sunflower Cookies

<table>
<tr><td>

INGREDIENTS

*1 cup shelled sunflower
seeds*
*½ cup safflower, soy, or
corn oil soft margarine*
*½ cup brown sugar, firmly
packed*
1 egg
*½ teaspoon almond ex-
tract*
*½ teaspoon vanilla ex-
tract*
1 cup whole wheat flour
1teaspoon baking powder
½ cup rolled oats

</td><td>

UTENSILS

measuring cups
skillet
wooden spoon
cooking spoons
heatproof measuring cup
*electric blender (see page
23)*
rubber spatula
waxed paper
bowl
measuring spoons
flour sifter
teaspoon
cookie sheets
sharp-tined fork
spatula or pancake turner
wire rack

</td></tr>
</table>

Put sunflower seeds in a skillet and set over medium flame. Stir with a wooden spoon until seeds become very light brown, about 5 minutes. Watch carefully and do not allow to become too brown or to make a popping noise. Remove skillet from heat.

Ask an adult to show you how your electric blender works. Spoon ½ cup of the sunflower seeds into a heatproof measuring cup, and pour them into the container of electric blender. Cover. Turn on blender and blend a few seconds until seeds are ground to a powder. Turn off. Remove cover and with rubber spatula scrape down any seeds from the sides that have not been ground. Put cover on again. Turn on blender again for a few seconds. Turn off. Remove cover. Scrape the powdered sunflower seeds out onto a sheet of waxed paper.

Turn on oven to heat at 350°. Grease cookie sheets. Cream margarine in a bowl until soft. Add brown sugar and mix until combined. Add egg, almond extract, and vanilla extract, and mix until thoroughly combined. Add the powdered sunflower seeds and mix again.

Sift flour and baking powder together. Add to the cookie dough and mix well. Add rolled oats and whole sunflower seeds from the skillet and mix until thoroughly combined.

Using a teaspoon, drop dough in generous spoonfuls on cookie sheets, leaving 2 or 3 inches between each cookie. Using a sharp-tined fork, flatten the cookies down, making criss-cross marks on the cookies with the fork. Bake 8 to 10 minutes or until very lightly browned around the edges. Remove from cookie sheets with spatula or pancake turner and cool on wire rack (see page 32).

Makes about 3½ dozen.

Banana Bumps

<table>
<tr><td>

INGREDIENTS

2 tablespoons safflower,
   soy, or corn oil soft mar-
   garine
4 bananas
¼ cup firmly packed
   brown sugar or tur-
   binado sugar
¼ teaspoon cinnamon
grated rind of 1 lemon
grated rind of 1 orange
¼ cup orange juice

</td><td>

UTENSILS
paring knife
small saucepan
pastry brush
measuring spoons
measuring cups
small bowl
shallow baking dish
shredder/grater (see page
   26)

</td></tr>
</table>

Turn on oven to heat at 350°.

Cut bananas into slices about ¾ inch wide and place in baking dish. Melt margarine in small saucepan over low heat and pour over the banana slices. Use a pastry brush to make sure they are covered all over with the margarine. Place in oven and bake 10 minutes.

While bananas are baking, grate the orange rind and lemon rind on the fine side of the grater. Mix together in a small bowl the sugar, cinnamon, grated rinds, and orange juice.

When bananas have baked for 10 minutes, remove from oven. Pour the orange juice mixture over them, coating them evenly with the pastry brush. Bake in oven for another 10 minutes. Serve immediately, or allow to cool slightly before serving.

Makes 4 servings.

Hint: If you have green bananas, the quickest way to get them ripe is to put them in a brown paper bag and keep them at room temperature until they turn yellow.

Peanut Date Squares

INGREDIENTS

½ *cup safflower, soy, or
corn oil soft margarine*
½ *cup honey*
1 egg
1 teaspoon vanilla extract
¾ *cup unbleached en-
riched white flour*
1 teaspoon baking powder
¼ *cup wheat germ*
¾ *cup chopped peanuts*
½ *cup chopped pitted
dates*

UTENSILS

*baking pan, 8 inches
square*
chef's knife
measuring cups
mixing bowl
cooking spoons
measuring spoons
flour sifter
rubber spatula
cake tester
wire rack
small sharp knife
pancake turner or spatula

Turn on oven to heat at 350°. Grease baking pan. Chop peanuts. Chop dates.

Cream margarine. Add honey and mix well. Add egg and vanilla and mix until well blended.

Sift the flour and baking powder together. Add to the margarine mixture along with wheat germ. Add peanuts and dates and mix until thoroughly blended.

Spread the dough evenly in the baking pan using a rubber spatula to smooth top. Bake about 25 minutes until a cake tester inserted in the center comes out clean. Make sure you don't stick the cake tester through a date, which will be sticky. Remove pan from oven and set on wire rack to cool. When cool,

cut into 2-inch squares. Remove from pan with pancake turner or spatula.

Makes 16 squares.

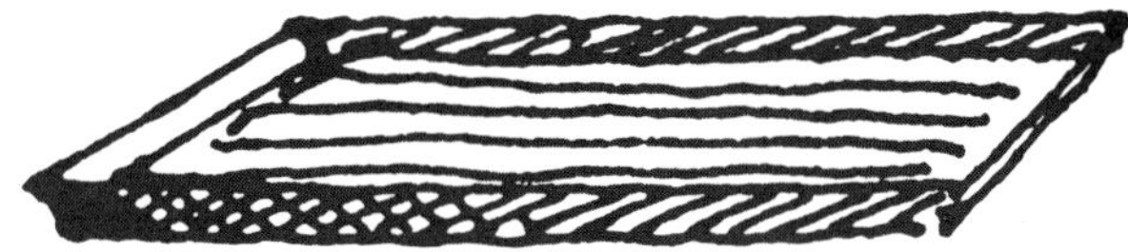

Saucy Apple Bake

INGREDIENTS

5 cups sliced apples (about
   4 medium-size apples)
juice of half a lemon
¼ cup turbinado sugar or
   firmly packed brown
   sugar
1 cup uncooked oatmeal
¼ cup turbinado sugar or
   firmly packed brown
   sugar
½ cup whole wheat flour
⅓ cup safflower, soy, or
   corn oil soft margarine

UTENSILS

apple corer
chef's knife
measuring cups
juice squeezer
baking dish, 8 inches
   square
bowl
pastry blender or paring
   knife

Turn on oven to heat at 350°. Grease baking dish. Wash apples, remove cores (see page 32), and slice enough apples to make 5 cups. Squeeze lemon.

Put sliced apples in baking dish and sprinkle with lemon juice and sugar. Mix together in a bowl oatmeal, sugar, and flour. Add margarine and blend with a pastry blender or paring knife until mixture is crumbly. Sprinkle over apples. Bake for 30 minutes or until top is crisp and brown. Serve warm or cold. If you wish, you can pour some cold milk or light cream over each serving.

Makes 4 to 6 servings.

You can make this recipe with fresh peaches instead of apples if you want to. Peel the peaches before you slice them.

Charlie Brownie Pudding

INGREDIENTS

FOR BATTER

½ cup whole wheat flour
1 teaspoon baking powder
½ teaspoon sea salt or
   iodized salt
⅓ cup turbinado sugar
1 tablespoon carob powder
¼ cup milk
1 tablespoon safflower,
   soy, or corn oil soft
   margarine
½ teaspoon vanilla ex-
   tract
¼ cup chopped nuts

UTENSILS

2 bowls
flour sifter
measuring cups
measuring spoons
cooking spoon
small saucepan
chef's knife
shallow round baking pan,
   7 inches in diameter or
   similar size
rubber spatula

INGREDIENTS

FOR TOPPING

½ cup firmly packed
   brown sugar
2 tablespoons carob pow-
   der
⅔ cup boiling water

Turn on oven to heat at 350°. Grease baking dish. Chop nuts.

Sift together flour, baking powder, salt, sugar, and carob powder. Melt margarine over low flame in a small saucepan, add to flour mixture with the milk and vanilla, and mix together just enough to combine. Add nuts and mix slightly. Pour into baking dish and spread it out evenly with a rubber spatula.

Topping: Mix together in a small bowl the brown sugar and carob powder. Sprinkle over the batter. *Do not stir it in*.

Gently pour the boiling water over top, but again *do not stir it in*. Carefully place the baking pan in oven and bake for 30 minutes.

Makes 6 servings.

Carrot Cake

INGREDIENTS	UTENSILS
½ cup safflower, soy, or corn oil soft margarine	bowl
½ cup honey	measuring cups
½ teaspoon cinnamon	measuring spoons
¼ teaspoon mace	cooking spoon
⅛ teaspoon sea salt or iodized salt	vegetable peeler
2 eggs	shredder / grater (see page 26)
1 cup coarsely grated carrots	chef's knife
½ cup chopped nuts	flour sifter
1¼ cups whole wheat flour	baking pan, 8 inches square
1½ teaspoons baking powder	cake tester
	wire rack

Turn on oven to heat at 350°. Grease baking pan. Sprinkle with a tablespoon of flour and shake the pan to coat it evenly with flour. Turn the pan over and knock out excess flour. Grate the carrots and chop the nuts.

Cream margarine in a bowl until soft. Add honey and mix well. Stir in cinnamon, mace, and salt. Add eggs and mix well. Add carrots and nuts and mix again.

Sift together flour and baking powder. Add to batter a little at a time, mixing well each time.

Pour batter into baking pan and bake 30 minutes until a cake tester inserted in center comes out clean. Remove from oven.

If you wish to frost the cake, do not remove it from the baking pan. Follow directions for Nut Chunk Frosting on page 123.

If you do not wish to frost the cake, turn it out of the baking pan onto wire rack to cool (see page 32). When cool, cut into squares and serve plain.

Nut Chunk Frosting

INGREDIENTS

4 tablespoons safflower,
   soy, or corn oil soft
   margarine
4 tablespoons honey
½ cup finely chopped nuts

UTENSILS

small saucepan
measuring cup
measuring spoons
cooking spoon
spatula or table knife

Turn on broiler to heat. Chop nuts.

Melt margarine in a small saucepan. Add honey and bring just to a boil. Remove from stove. Add nuts and stir into honey mixture. Spread on top of baked Carrot Cake in its baking pan, using a spatula or round-ended table knife to spread evenly.

Place cake pan under broiler for 1 minute. Remove from oven and set pan on wire rack.

Serve warm or cool. You can cut the cake into squares and serve it right from the pan.

SNACKS
AND CANDY

Sesame Break-Up

INGREDIENTS	UTENSILS
1 cup turbinado sugar	*aluminum foil*
1 tablespoon peanut, safflower, or sesame oil	*measuring cup*
	measuring spoons
pinch of sea salt or iodized salt	*large frying pan*
	cooking spoon
1 cup sesame seeds	*spatula*

Rub some oil on one side of a 14-inch-long piece of aluminum foil.

Place sugar, oil, and salt in frying pan and place over medium heat. Stir constantly until sugar is completely melted, about 7 to 8 minutes. It will be brown and syrupy. Remove from heat and stir in sesame seeds. Turn mixture out onto the oiled aluminum foil and spread it out with a spatula. Allow to cool.

Peel off the foil and break the candy into pieces.

Hint: If you want to vary this recipe, you can use sunflower seeds or pumpkin seeds with the sesame seeds. Or mix them up any way you like—just so long as you use one cup of seeds.

Yum Yogurt Pops

<table>
<tr><td>INGREDIENTS</td><td>UTENSILS</td></tr>
<tr><td>2 cups plain yogurt</td><td>chef's knife</td></tr>
<tr><td>2 tablespoons wheat germ</td><td>bowl</td></tr>
<tr><td>2 tablespoons chopped
   dates or raisins</td><td>measuring cups</td></tr>
<tr><td>2 tablespoons chopped
   nuts</td><td>measuring spoons</td></tr>
<tr><td>¼ cup jam (any flavor you
   like, such as Tutti-
   Frutti [see page 132] or
   strawberry)</td><td>cooking spoon
6 to 8 small paper or plas-
   tic cups
6 to 8 ice-cream sticks or
   plastic spoons</td></tr>
</table>

Chop the nuts and the dates or raisins. Empty yogurt into a bowl and stir until smooth. Add wheat germ, dates or raisins, and nuts, and mix. Add jam and stir slightly so that jam makes a swirling pattern in the yogurt.

Spoon into small paper or plastic cups and place in freezing compartment in refrigerator. When partly frozen (about 30 minutes), insert an ice-cream stick or plastic spoon into each cup of yogurt to form a handle.

Continue to freeze until hard, from 2 to 4 hours.

Remove yogurt pops from cups by pushing firmly on the bottoms of the cups.

Makes 6 to 8 pops.

Rye Crackers

<table>
<tr><td>

INGREDIENTS

1 cup rye flour
¼ cup soy flour
*¼ cup nonfat dry milk
  powder*
¼ cup wheat germ
*¼ teaspoon sea salt or
  iodized salt*
1 teaspoon baking powder
*½ cup safflower, soy, or
  corn oil soft margarine*
¼ cup milk

</td><td>

UTENSILS

measuring cups
cookie sheets
bowl
measuring spoons
cooking spoon
table knife
pastry blender
pastry board
*plastic wrap or waxed
  paper*
rolling pin
*pizza cutter, pastry wheel,
  or small sharp knife*
pancake turner or spatula
table fork
wire rack

</td></tr>
</table>

Measure margarine and put in freezer for 30 minutes. Turn on oven to heat at 350°. Grease cookie sheets.

Combine rye flour, soy flour, dry milk powder, wheat germ, salt, and baking powder in a bowl. Remove margarine from freezer. Cut into pieces and drop into the flour mixture. With a spoon toss the flour mixture over the margarine. With a pastry blender blend the margarine into the flour mixture using a downward chopping and twisting motion. The mixture should look like coarse meal when you are finished. Add milk and stir in quickly with a spoon. Blend well.

Form dough into a ball with your hands. Wrap in plastic wrap or waxed paper and put in freezer 15 minutes.

Sprinkle some flour on a pastry board or wooden work-table top. Put the dough onto the flour and flatten it as much as you can with your hands. Then roll it out with a floured rolling pin. Keep flouring the rolling pin and roll until the dough is as thin as you can make it. Cut into 2-inch squares with a pizza cutter, pastry wheel, or small sharp knife, or cut into any shape you like. Transfer the squares to cookie sheets with a pancake turner or spatula. Prick each square several times with the tines of a fork to make a row of marks.

Bake 8 minutes. Remove cookie sheets from oven. Turn the crackers over with a pancake turner or spatula. Put the cookie sheets back in the oven and bake another 2 minutes. Remove from oven and with pancake turner or spatula, turn the crackers right side up, and transfer them to a wire rack to cool.

Makes about 3 dozen.

Chi-Chi Dip

INGREDIENTS	UTENSILS
1 15- or 16-ounce can chick peas (garbanzos) or 1¾ to 2 cups cooked chick peas (see page 30)	*lemon squeezer*
6 tablespoons lemon juice	*paring knife*
2 cloves garlic, chopped	*strainer*
½ teaspoon sea salt or iodized salt	*measuring cup*
dash of paprika	*2 bowls*
½ cup tahini (ground sesame seed)	*electric blender (see page 23)*
	measuring spoons
	cooking spoon
	rubber spatula

Squeeze lemon juice. Chop garlic. Drain and measure chick peas, reserving ¼ to ½ cup of the liquid in a bowl.

Ask an adult to show you how to use your electric blender. Place chick peas, lemon juice, garlic, salt, paprika, tahini, and ¼ cup of the reserved liquid in the container of an electric blender. Cover and blend well. Turn off blender and remove cover. Scrape down sides with rubber spatula. If necessary, add more of the reserved liquid so that the mixture is the consistency of creamy mayonnaise. Cover and blend again. Turn off blender and remove cover. Scrape the dip into a bowl. Cover and chill in refrigerator 1 hour or longer.

Use as a dip with raw vegetables, whole grain wafers, pita bread, or Rye Crackers (see page 128).

Makes about 2½ cups.

Hint: If you want to serve the dip at a party, it looks nice to sprinkle a few teaspoons of chopped fresh parsley on it.

Tutti-Frutti Jam

INGREDIENTS
1 orange
1 lemon
½ cup pitted dates
¾ cup pitted prunes
¾ cup raisins
½ cup dried apricots
½ cup dried figs
1¼ cups water

UTENSILS
chef's knife
measuring cups
saucepan
cooking spoons
meat grinder (see page 25)
bowl
3 half-pint jars with tight
  lids

Wash and dry orange and lemon and cut them into ¼-inch slices. Remove any pits. Combine slices in a saucepan with dates, prunes, raisins, apricots, figs, and water. Place over medium heat and bring to boil. Lower heat, cover, and simmer 30 minutes, stirring occasionally. If liquid is not all absorbed, remove cover, raise heat to medium, and cook a few minutes, stirring constantly, until most of liquid is gone. Remove saucepan from stove and remove cover. Allow to cool.

When fruit is cool, put it through a meat grinder with a medium-size blade, letting ground fruit drop into a bowl. Mix thoroughly with a spoon. Pack into glass jars and cover tightly. Keep in refrigerator until you want to have some jam.

Makes about 3 cups.

Cheese Quicks

<table>
<tr><td>

INGREDIENTS

*2 tablespoons safflower,
  soy, or corn oil soft
  margarine*
*1⅓ cups grated Cheddar,
  Monterey Jack, or
  muenster cheese (about
  ¼ pound)*
*1 loaf unsliced Two Grain
  Bread (see page 103), or
  whole wheat bread*

</td><td>

UTENSILS

measuring cup
measuring spoons
small bowl
cooking spoon
*shredder/grater (see page
  26)*
bread knife
2 clean dish towels
spreader or table knife
plastic wrap
chef's knife
cookie sheet
spatula or pancake turner

</td></tr>
</table>

Grate the cheese. Cream margarine in a small bowl until soft. Add grated cheese and mix well.

Cut lengthwise 3 or 4 very thin slices from the unsliced bread. Trim off crusts evenly and save them to use as bread crumbs in another recipe. Wet and wring out a clean dish towel and lay the slices on it. Put another damp dish towel over the slices and allow them to stand for 10 minutes. Remove the top towel.

Spread the slices with the cheese mixture and roll up each slice like a jelly roll. Don't worry if the bread breaks a little. Wrap the rolls very tightly in plastic wrap and place them in the refrigerator 2 hours or longer. You can do this a day ahead if you like.

When ready for a snack, turn on broiler to heat. Remove rolls from refrigerator and take off plastic wrap. Slice into half-inch slices and arrange on a cookie sheet.

Place under broiler for about 2 minutes or until brown and bubbly. Remove from oven and transfer Cheese Quicks to a serving dish with a spatula or pancake turner.

Makes 24 or more pieces.

DRINKS

Pink Wink

INGREDIENTS

1 egg
1 cup ice-cold milk
*1 cup ice-cold cranberry
  juice*
*1 tablespoon strawberry
  or raspberry pure fruit
  syrup*
1 teaspoon honey

UTENSILS

bowl
egg beater
measuring cup
measuring spoons

Beat egg in a bowl with egg beater. Add milk, cranberry juice, fruit syrup, and honey. Beat again.

Pour into 2 glasses.

Makes 2 servings. If you want to make 4 servings, double all the ingredients and make the same way.

Fruit Whizz

<table>
<tr><td>

INGREDIENTS

1 cup ice-cold milk
1 sliced banana
1 tablespoon wheat germ
*½ cup ice-cold orange
    juice*
1 teaspoon honey
*½ cup ice-cold un-
    sweetened pineapple
    juice*

</td><td>

UTENSILS

*electric blender (see page
    23)*
measuring cup
measuring spoons
paring knife

</td></tr>
</table>

Ask an adult to show you how to use your electric blender.

Place milk and sliced banana in container of electric blender. Cover. Turn on blender and blend at high speed for 5 seconds. Turn off. Remove cover. Pour in wheat germ, orange juice, honey, and pineapple juice. Cover. Blend 5 seconds more. Turn off. Remove cover and pour into 2 glasses.

Makes 2 servings.

INGREDIENTS

2 *eggs at room tempera-
ture*
¼ *cup milk at room tem-
perature*
3 *tablespoons carob pow-
der*
*pinch of sea salt or iodized
salt*
¼ *teaspoon vanilla ex-
tract*
1¼ *cups milk*
1 *tablespoon brown sugar
or turbinado sugar*
*finely grated coconut
(optional)*

UTENSILS

small bowl
egg beater
measuring cup
measuring spoons
small saucepan
cooking spoon

In a bowl beat the eggs until very foamy. Beat in the ¼ cup milk and vanilla extract. Beat in the carob powder and salt.

In a small saucepan combine 1¼ cups milk and the sugar. Stir over medium heat just to boiling point. Remove from heat and beat into the egg mixture with egg beater. Pour into 2 cups.

If you like, sprinkle a little finely grated coconut over each cup.

Makes 2 servings.

Temperature Conversion

The temperatures shown throughout this book are in degrees Fahrenheit. If you want to use degrees Centigrade (Celsius) look for the correct temperature conversion below:

FAHRENHEIT	CENTIGRADE (CELSIUS)
115°	46°
150°	65°
250°	121°
300°	149°
325°	163°
350°	177°
375°	191°

Index